INDONESIAN

SURVIVAL
INDONESIAN

How to communicate without fuss or fear INSTANTLY!

by Katherine Davidsen

TUTTLE Publishing

Tokyo | Rutland, Vermont | Singapore

CONTENTS

INTRODUCTION AND PRONUNCIATION GUIDE

Welcome to Indonesian! This logical, practical language will be of great use to you not only in the Republic of Indonesia, but also Malaysia, Brunei and even Singapore. A few words and, more importantly, a desire to communicate and understand will endear you to young and old, hotel reception staff, waiters, fellow bus passengers, rickshaw drivers, children, shopkeepers, swaggering teenagers and university students, to name a few.

Background to Indonesian

Indonesian is one of four modern languages created in the twentieth century which now have the status of a national language and are used as a medium in higher education (the others are Afrikaans, Hebrew and Hindi). Based on Malay, to which it is obviously very similar, Indonesian is widely understood (if not necessarily spoken) across Southeast Asia in Malaysia, Brunei, Singapore, East Timor and even parts of southern Thailand. Malay was the language of trade throughout pre-colonial and Dutch times from Sumatra and the Malay peninsula in the west to the Spice Islands (present-day Maluku) and beyond in the east. This widespread usage was one reason for its adoption by the independence movement in Indonesia in the 1930s who, upon freedom in 1945, then made it the national language of the fledgling state.

Indonesian is sometimes mistakenly referred to as "Bahasa." *Bahasa Indonesia* simply means "Indonesian language," which is the common language of all Indonesians, whether their first language is Javanese *(bahasa Jawa)*, Sundanese *(bahasa Sunda)* or one of the other 700 regional languages spoken across the archipelago. It is written in the Latin alphabet and is phonetic, which makes it easy to learn. Its grammar is also relatively logical, as will be explained.

Pronunciation Guide

The pronunciation of Indonesian is regular once you learn a few sounds particular to the language (shown here with an *). In general, the sounds of Indonesian are similar to that of Italian or Spanish.

a   as in *Bali, father*. Never "ay" as in English
e   as in *mother* (unvoiced shwa sound)
e + accent (**é**, usually not written) as in **saté**, **café**. This sound is much less common than the unvoiced **e**. In this book, an accent will be shown, but this does not appear in ordinary written Indonesian. Neither **e** nor **é** is ever pronounced as "ee" like in English.

i	as in *mini*, *piano*. Never "eye" as in English.
o	as in *pogo*, *piano*
u	as in *ukulele*, *true*
b	as in *bed*, *Bali*
c*	as in *chair*, *church* (never k in words of Indonesian origin)
d	as in *door*, *diva*
f	as in *five*, *off* (some Indonesians say *p* instead of *f*)
g	as in *goat*, *giggle* (always hard)
h	as in *hello*
j	as in *juice*, *Jakarta*
k	as in *kettle*, *Kalimantan*
l	as in *lemon*
m	as in *Médan*, *mini*
n	as in *November*
ng*	as in *singing*, *gong*
ngg*	as in *finger* (**ng** + **g**)
p	as in *party*, *pen*
q	is only in words of Arabic origin and is pronounced *k*, e.g. *Qatar*
r*	is trilled as in Spanish. *Rrrrr*. A tricky sound to learn.
s	as in *sarong*, *satay*
t	as in *tornado*, *tent*
v*	is pronounced as *f*, usually in words from Dutch, e.g. the female name Vivi is usually pronounced *Fifi*.

w   as in <u>w</u>ater, <u>W</u>ednesday
y   as in <u>y</u>ellow, <u>y</u>oung
z   as in <u>z</u>oo. This letter is not common and is pro-
         nounced as *j* by some people.

The alphabet can be sung to the same tune as the English alphabet song:

Ah bé sé dé é éf gé
Ha ii jé ka él ém én
O pé ki érr éss té oo
Fé wé éks yé zét

The International Phonetic Alphabet is very useful where it is unclear whether the English or Indonesian alphabet is being used. Misspelt international airline tickets can cause a great deal of problems and stress, so make sure you always check spelling and name order. The concept of having a family name is a fairly recent development and the idea of surnames is quite unfamiliar to even some westernized Indonesians.

The following codes are used for Indonesian letters and numbers when given verbally (e.g. over a phone):

Alpha bravo Charlie delta echo foxtrot golf hotel
India Juliet kilo London (the usual equivalent
is Lima, but this means 5 in Indonesian) Mike

November Oscar Papa Quebec Romeo sierra tango uniform victor whiskey x-ray Yankee Zulu

Numbers are said by putting the word **angka** (number) before the actual number. For example: IP32AF would be read

ii / peh / angka tiga / angka dua / ah / eff,

or

India / Papa / angka tiga / angka dua / alpha / foxtrot.

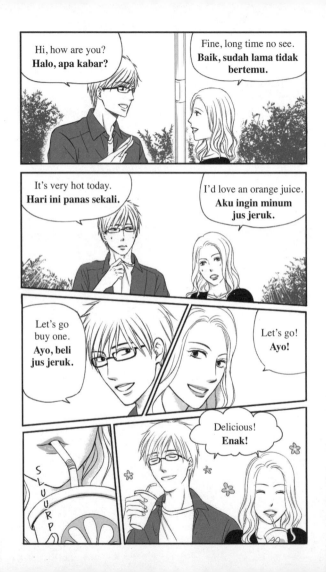

PART ONE
Essential Language Pointers

This is essential reading to get an overview before you begin trying out phrases.

Indonesian word order is basically the same as English but can be flexible, i.e. subject / verb / object.

Saya makan nasi.
I   eat   rice.

One key difference is that adjectives follow the noun, as in French, e.g.

Saya makan nasi putih.
I   eat   rice   white.   (= I eat white rice.)

One great feature is that, unlike in English, you do not have to worry about tense, plural or gender. When these are shown, they are done so in other, more intuitive ways.

PRONOUNS

SINGULAR

I	**saya, aku** (informally or to children)

you   usually not stated. You can use **anda** (a bit stilted) or the person's name. **Kamu** is very familiar or for children. **Engkau** or **kau** is common in Sumatra.

he, she, it   **dia**

PLURAL

we   **kita** (including person being addressed), **kami** (excluding person being addressed)

you   **kalian**. This is a useful word which is neither distant or over-familiar.

they   **meréka**

These can all be used as adjectives to create possessive pronouns, e.g.

buku saya my book   **buku kita** our book

Sometimes these are abbreviated.

I
aku

you
kamu

she
dia

he
dia

it
dia

we
kita

we
kami

you (plural)
kalian

they
mereka

bukunya   (from **buku dia**) his or her book, the book
bukumu   your (familiar) book
bukuku   my (familiar) book

Sometimes pronouns are omitted in spoken Indonesian, especially when referring to other people, or if who you are referring to is clear from the context of the sentence.

NOUNS

These always come before any adjective describing them, except when counting.

tas   bag
tas biru   blue bag

bis   bus
bis biru   blue bus

uang   money
tiga tas biru three blue bags

Many words with the affixes **ke-an** are nouns, often with a more abstract meaning.

uang money; **keuangan** finance
aman secure, safe; **keamanan** security

Per-an is another affix denoting more abstract nouns.

tani farmer; **<u>pertanian</u>** agriculture
usaha trade, business; **<u>perusahaan</u>** company

ADJECTIVES

These always follow the noun (or verb) they describe.
There is no clear distinction between adjectives and adverbs (which describe verbs).

biru	blue
tas biru	blue bag
besar	big
tas besar	big bag
lama	long, slow, old (of time)
tas lama	old bag
baik	good, well (of people, situations)
tas bagus	good bag

VERBS

Indonesian is very rich in action words or verbs. There
are single words to describe an action using a number of
English words, e.g.

| **mengamuk** | having a tantrum |
| **mengupil** | picking your nose |

Simple, common words include:

makan	eat
minum	drink
datang	come
pergi	go
naik	ride on, go up
tidur	sleep

More sophisticated meaning can be found in verbs beginning with **meN-** (where **N-** represents a variety of possible nasal-sounding endings). Such verbs may end in the suffix **-kan** (which may denote an object or doing something for someone) or **-i** (which may suggest repetition or an object which is human).

| <u>**men</u>datang<u>kan**</u> | to import (i.e. to bring something to) |
| **menaik<u>i</u>** | to ride on (a vehicle) |

The **meN-** prefix changes according to the base word following it. You will learn these through experience rather than trying to memorize the rule.

| **me-** before *l, m, n, r, w, y* | **melihat, memakan, menaiki, merusakkan, mewarnai, meyakini** |

mem- before *b, f, v*	**membuka, memfokus, memvonis**
men- before *c, d, j*	**mencuci, mendaki, menjemur**
meng- before all vowels *(a e i o u), g, h*	**mengaku, menggigit, menghias**
before *k*, **meN-** becomes **meng** (the **k** disappears)	**kawin → mengawinkan**
before *p*, **meN-** becomes **mem** (the *p* disappears)	**panas → memanaskan**
before *s*, **meN-** becomes **meny** (the *s* disappears)	**suka → menyukai**
before *t*, **meN-** becomes **men** (the *t* disappears)	**tidur → menidurkan**

There are a number of tense markers that behave like **auxiliary verbs**, which are very useful. They often show when something has happened or will happen.

sudah, telah (more formal)	already
belum	not yet
tidak	not
bukan	not (of an object)
sedang, lagi (informal)	in the process of
akan	will
mau	want to, will
bisa	can
boléh	allowed, permitted
tidak boléh	not allowed

▶ Have you eaten?
   Sudah makan?

▶ Not yet.
   Belum

▶ I'm eating.
   Sedang makan.

▶ I'm going to.
   Mau.

▶ May I eat?
   Boléh makan?

ADVERBS

To describe how someone is doing something, add **dengan** (*with*) or **secara** (*in the way of*) before the word you are describing. This is like adding *-ly* to English adjectives to make them adverbs, e.g.

Dia	**makan**	**dengan**	**lapar.**
She	eats	with	hunger.

(= she eats hungrily)

Sari	**menyetrika**	**secara**	**hati-hati.**
Sari	irons	in the way of	careful

(= Sari irons carefully.)

You can often leave out **dengan** or **secara**.

Sari	**hati-hati**	**menyetrika.**
Sari	careful	to iron. (= Sari irons carefully.)

PREPOSITIONS

The most common preposition is **di** (*in, at*).

Di mana?	**Di Jakarta**
Where?	In Jakarta

This is a separate word, and not attached like the prefix **di-**, which makes a verb passive.

Dilarang	**merokok**	**di**	**kamar kecil.**
Forbidden	smoking	in	toilet.

(= No smoking in the toilet)

For time, **pada** (*in, on*) is very useful.

pada jam 10	at 10 o'clock
pada hari Senin	on Monday
pada bulan Juni	in June
pada tahun 2014	in 2014

You may also hear **di** for time, but this is slangy and less grammatical.

to	**ke**	from	**dari**

Almost all other prepositions can take **di** before them.

on	**di (atas)**	in front of	**(di) depan**
over	**di atas**	next to	**di samping**
under	**di bawah**	within	**di dalam**
between	**(di) antara**	around	**di sekitar**
beside	**di sebelah**	near	**di dekat**
behind	**di belakang**		

NUMBERS

These are regular and logical. This should be one of the first vocabulary sets you learn!

1	**satu**
2	**dua**
3	**tiga**
4	**empat**
5	**lima**
6	**enam**
7	**tujuh**
8	**delapan**
9	**sembilan**
10	**sepuluh** (lit. **satu puluh** or one ten)

For the numbers 11 to 19 add **belas** (= teen):

11	**sebelas (satu belas)**
12	**dua belas**
13	**tiga belas**, etc.

For numbers ending in -0 add **puluh** (= ten):

20	**dua puluh**
30	**tiga puluh**
40	**empat puluh**
50	**lima puluh**

Bigger numbers:

100	**seratus** (= satu ratus)
200	**dua ratus**
500	**lima ratus**
1.000	**seribu** (= satu ribu)
2.000	**dua ribu**
10.000	**sepuluh ribu**
50.000	**lima puluh ribu**
100.000	**seratus ribu**
1.000.000	**sejuta** (= satu juta)
2.000.000	**dua juta**

You will notice that traditionally full stops are used to divide up thousand values. Increasingly you will see commas, as in English, but particularly with money, full stops are still the official format.

Ordinal numbers are very regular (except for one "the first") – just add **ke-** to the number, however large:

1st	**pertama**
2nd	**kedua**
3rd	**ketiga**
4th	**keempat**
5th	**kelima**
20th	**keduapuluh**

Decimals are as in English, but use a comma rather than a full stop. So 4.5 (four point five) is 4,5 (**empat koma lima**) in Indonesian.

½ (one half)	**setengah, separuh**
⅓ (one third)	**sepertiga**
⅔ (two thirds)	**dua pertiga**
¼ (one quarter)	**seperempat**
¾ (three quarters)	**tiga perempat**

COUNTERS

Like many Asian languages, Indonesian often uses a counter word when talking about a number of objects. This is similar to the English use of "twenty head of cattle," "six pairs of pants" etc.

If you leave them out, people will still understand you, but you will hear them used and you will speak better Indonesian if you can use them.

orang   for people, e.g. **dua orang bayi** two babies

buah   fruit, general counter for largish objects,
                e.g. **lima buah jeruk** five oranges; **empat
                buah mobil** four cars

biji   seed, general counter for small objects, e.g.
                tiga biji kancing three buttons

ékor   for animals, e.g. **seékor sapi** a cow
batang   for long thin objects, e.g. **sepuluh batang
                rokok** ten cigarettes

ASKING QUESTIONS

who	**siapa**
what	**apa**
where	**di mana,** (directional) **ke mana**
when	**kapan**
how	**bagaimana**
why	**mengapa, kenapa** (colloquial)
yes	**ya**
no	**tidak, bukan** (for objects)
not yet	**belum**

To make a question not using a question word, all you have to do is start the sentence with **Apakah** (or **Apa** for short). Literally, **apakah** means "whether" while **apa** means "what."

▶ Joni likes eating crab.
  Joni suka makan kepiting.

▶ Does Joni like eating crab?
  Apakah Joni suka makan kepiting?

▶ It's too hot.
  Kepanasan.

▶ Is it too hot?
  Apa kepanasan?

As in English, you can simply use a rising intonation at the end of the sentence to make it a question, but it is much simpler and clearer to use **Apa** or **Apakah** in front.

PART TWO
Key Words and Expressions

INTRODUCTIONS & SMALL TALK

Good morning	
(until 10 a.m. or so)	**Selamat pagi**
(from 10 to midday)	**Selamat siang**
Good afternoon	
(from midday to 3 p.m.)	**Selamat siang**
(from 3 p.m. to dark)	**Selamat soré**
Good evening	**Selamat malam**
Good night	**Selamat tidur**

▶ Hello (more informal)
  Halo

▶ How are you?
  Apa kabar? (lit. what news?)

▶ Fine
  Kabar baik (lit. news good)
  Baik-baik saja (lit. just OK)

Times of the day are divided into three phases in Indonesia: **pagi**, **siang** and **soré**.

Communicating

▶ Do you speak English?
  Apa bisa bahasa Inggris?

▶ Yes, a bit.
  Bisa, sedikit.

▶ I can speak English.
  Saya bisa berbahasa Inggris.

English	**bahasa Inggris**
Indonesian	**Bahasa Indonesia**
Dutch	**bahasa Belanda**
Javanese	**bahasa Jawa**

▶ Can you speak slowly please?
  Tolong bicara perlahan-lahan.

▶ Can you say it again?
  Tolong, sekali lagi.

▶ I understand.
  Saya mengerti.

▶ I don't understand.
  Saya tidak mengerti.

▶ I want to learn Indonesian.
Saya mau belajar Bahasa Indonesia.

Excuse me	**Permisi**
Sorry	**Maaf**
Thank you	**Terima kasih**
You're welcome/	**Sama-sama / (Terima kasih)**
That's OK	**kembali**
No, thank you	**Terima kasih**
Please	**Tolong** (asking for help)
	Coba (if inviting someone to try something)
	Silahkan (if offering something)

▶ I'm going now.
Mari, saya duluan ya.

Goodbye	**Mari / Silahkan**
Goodbye (have a good trip)	**Selamat jalan**
Goodbye (to someone staying)	**Selamat tinggal**

It is important to take leave of others. Indonesians would not leave the house without saying goodbye first (**pamit**) to those staying behind, especially if they are older. This is also the case if you have chatted with someone. It is very good manners to do it after you have paid for something.

Small Talk

Indonesians are very fond of asking questions, some of which might seem rather personal to Westerners. You shouldn't be offended as you might back home. Answer those that you can, and ask the same question back! Alternatively you can give vague answers—nobody is that interested in the accuracy of your response, they just want to chat.

▶ Where are you going?
Mau ke mana? (lit. want to where?)

This is a very common question and people may not be really interested in your answer. It is a bit like commenting on the weather in English.

▶ Just having a wander.
Jalan-jalan saja. (lit. just going around)

▶ To the market.
Mau ke pasar.

▶ To the beach.
Mau ke pantai.

▶ Have you been here long?
Sudah lama di sini?

▶ Just two days
 Baru dua hari.

▶ Already a week.
 Sudah seminggu.

▶ Two months.
 Dua bulan.

▶ Where are you from?
 Dari mana? (lit. from where?)

This could also mean, "Where have you just come from?" (ie. what was your last destination before here?) but when addressed to foreigners, it is usually asking about their origins.

▶ From America / the US.
 Dari Amérika.

▶ From Australia.
 Dari Australia.

▶ From Surabaya.
 Dari Surabaya.

Talking about Yourself

mother	**ibu**
father	**ayah**
older sister/brother	**kakak**
younger sister/brother	**adik**
husband	**suami**
wife	**isteri**
friend	**kawan, teman**
boyfriend/girlfriend	**pacar**

▶ What's your name?
Siapa namanya?

▶ My name's Rita.
Nama saya Rita.

▶ Who's this?
Ini siapa?

▶ This is my friend.
Ini kawan saya.

▶ This is my sibling / cousin / family member.
Ini saudara saya.

Indonesian society is still very traditional. It is better
to introduce a partner as a friend, unless you are
already married. This is also the case for same-sex

relationships. Indonesians in the same situation would do the same.

► Where do you live?
Tinggal di mana?

► I live in ...
Saya tinggal di ...

► What do you do (for a living)?
Kerja di mana?

► I'm a student.
Saya mahasiswa.

► I'm a doctor.
Saya dokter.

► I'm unemployed.
Saya sedang tidak bekerja.
(lit. I'm not working right now).

► How many brothers and sisters do you have?
Berapa bersaudara?

► I have ... older siblings and one younger sibling.
Saya ada ... orang kakak dan seorang adik.

▶ There are four of us altogether.
Kami bersaudara empat.

Indonesians focus on whether siblings are older or younger, rather than whether they are sisters or brothers.

▶ Are your parents still alive?
Apa orang tua masih ada?

▶ Both are still alive.
Dua-duanya masih ada.

▶ My mother is but not my father.
Ibu masih ada, tapi Bapak sudah tidak.

▶ No, not any more.
Sudah tidak ada.

▶ Are you married?
Apa sudah menikah?

▶ Yes.
Sudah.

▶ No.
Belum.

▶ I'm divorced.
  Sudah cerai.

Belum is literally (not yet). To say **tidak** would suggest you are philosophically anti-marriage, or are very pessimistic.

Unless you know the person well, better to simply say **belum nikah** to avoid going into details. Divorce is something of a taboo topic.

▶ How old are you?
  Umurnya berapa?

▶ I'm 32 (years old).
  Tiga puluh dua (tahun).

▶ I'm already old.
  Saya sudah tua.

▶ I'm still young.
  Saya masih muda.

Most people are very matter-of-fact about their age. Older people are greatly respected in Indonesian society—if you are usually embarrassed about your age, you may want to enjoy being more revered than you are back home. Giving an ambiguous answer will also provide amusement!

OUT & ABOUT

Arriving

Most international traffic in Indonesia is via air. The largest international airports are in Jakarta (Bandara Soekarno-Hatta) and Denpasar, Bali (Bandara Ngurah Rai) but there are also international flights to Medan, Padang, Manado and other regional centers.

There is a frequent ferry service from the island of Batam to Singapore, which runs several times a day, by various operators.

There are also land border crossings in Kalimantan, from East Malaysia, by bus. These are popular with Indonesian migrant workers earning Malaysian ringgit across the border in Sarawak or Sabah.

Visa requirements change frequently so be sure to check requirements for nationals of your country. Currently, many foreigners can obtain a visa on arrival with fairly little fuss for US$35 (new, clean bills).

ticket	**tikét**
luggage, baggage	**bagasi**
carry-on bags	**bagasi kabin**
checked-in luggage	**bagasi (di bawah)**
departure	**keberangkatan**
arrival	**kedatangan**
baggage collection	**tempat mengambil bagasi**
carousel	**korsél**

porter	**kuli**
piece of baggage	**koli**
three pieces of baggage	**tiga koli**
kilogram	**kilo**
four kilograms	**empat kilo**
suitcase	**koper**
bag	**tas**
trolley	**keréta, troli**
oversized baggage	**bagasi besar**
taxi	**taksi**
metered taxi	**taksi argo**
public bus	**bis umum**
hire car	**mobil séwa**
connecting flight	**penerbangan berikut, penerbangan lanjutan**
toilet	**kamar kecil, WC** [*we se*], **toilét**
ATM	**ATM** [*ah te em*]

▶ Where can I collect my baggage?
  Di mana mengambil bagasi?

▶ I have three pieces of baggage.
  Saya ada bagasi tiga koli.

▶ Where is my baggage?
  Di mana bagasi saya?

▶ My baggage is lost.
   Bagasi saya tidak ada. / Bagasi saya hilang.

▶ I have a baggage receipt.
   Saya ada struk bagasi.

▶ Is there a porter service?
   Ada jasa kuli?

▶ Where is the transfer desk?
   Di mana méja pindah pesawat?

▶ I have a connecting flight to ... .
   Saya mau terbang lagi ke ... .

▶ Do I need to collect my bags first?
   Apa harus mengambil bagasi dulu?

▶ Is my luggage checked through to my final
   destination?
   **Apa bagasi saya sudah langsung dikirim ke
   tujuan terakhir?**

▶ Can I please have an aisle / window seat?
   Minta duduk di lorong / di jendéla.

▶ Can we please sit together?
   Kami minta duduk bersama.

▶ Could we please have a baby bassinet?
Minta basinét buat bayi.

▶ I have a frequent flyer card.
Saya punya kartu anggota.

▶ When is the next flight to ... ?
Kapan pesawat berikutnya ke ... ?

▶ Is there an airport hotel?
Apakah ada hotél di bandara?

▶ Is there anywhere I can get something to eat / drink?
Di mana bisa beli makanan / minuman?

Accommodation

big	**besar**
small	**kecil**
cheap	**murah**
expensive	**mahal**
good	**bagus**
homestay	**losmén**
budget hotel	**hotél melati**
three-star	**bintang tiga**
four-star	**bintang empat**
five-star	**bintang lima**
bathroom	**kamar mandi**
hot running water	**air panas (buat mandi)**

Welcome.
Selamat datang.

Do you have a room available?
Apa masih ada kamar?

Yes, which type of room would you like?
Masih ada. Mau tipe kamar yang mana?

I'd like a room with a single bed.
Ada kamar dengan satu tempat tidur?

We have a room.
Ada.

I'll take one then. What time is breakfast?
Saya mau satu kamar kalau begitu. Jam berapa sarapan?

From 7 a.m. to 10 a.m.
Sarapan dari jam 7 sampai dengan jam 10.

blanket	**selimut**
laundry service	**cuci baju**
check in	**cék in, masuk**
check out	**cék out, keluar**
front desk	**resépsi, méja depan**
room rate	**tarif kamar**
swimming pool	**kolam renang**
stairs	**tangga**
elevator	**lift**
restaurant	**réstoran**
Internet access	**aksés ke internét**
business center	**pusat bisnis, warnét** (internét cafe)
English-language newspaper	**koran berbahasa Inggris**
key	**kunci**

▶ I have a reservation, in the name of ...
   Saya ada buking / résérvasi atas nama ...

▶ I booked it ... days ago.
   Saya sudah buking ... hari yang lalu.

▶ I'm looking for a cheap hotel.
   Saya mencari hotél murah.

▶ Do you know a good hotel?
   Hotél mana yang bagus?

▶ Do you have a room?
Ada kamar?

▶ What is the rate per night?
Tarif per malam berapa?

▶ For .... nights.
Untuk ... malam.

▶ I'd like a room ...
Ada kamar ... ?

with aircon	**dengan AC** [*ah seh*]
with a fan	**dengan kipas (angin)**
with a view	**dengan pemandangan**
with a single bed	**dengan satu tempat tidur**
with two beds	**dengan dua tempat tidur**
on the ground floor	**di lantai bawah**
on the first floor	**di lantai dua**

▶ Do you have a bigger room?
Ada kamar yang lebih besar?

▶ Does it include breakfast?
Apa termasuk sarapan?

▶ I have some laundry.
Saya ada baju untuk dicuci.

▶ Do you have ... ?
   Ada ... ?

▶ I want ...
   Saya mau ...

a double bed	**satu tempat tidur yang besar**
twin beds	**dua tempat tidur yang kecil**
air-conditioning	**AC** [*ah-se*]
a ceiling fan	**kipas angin**
cable TV	**TV kabel / parabola / luar**

▶ What time can we check in?
   Jam berapa bisa masuk kamar?

▶ What time do we check out?
   Jam berapa harus cek out?

▶ What time is breakfast?
   Sarapan jam berapa?

▶ Do you have any discounts?
   Apa bisa dapat diskon?

▶ Can you pick us up from the ... ?
Apa bisa dijemput dari ... ?

airport	**bandara**
station	**setasiun**
bus terminal	**terminal**
from the first to the ninth (dates)	**mulai tanggal satu sampai tanggal sembilan**

Indonesian hotels are usually excellent value for money. If you feel the room rate is excessive, try asking for a discount (**Ada diskon?**) You might get lucky.

You will usually be asked for identity when checking in—a passport is fine, or local driving licence or residence permit.

Nearly all hotels, however small, will be able to provide you with at least a thermos of hot water and cups for drinking. If one is not visible in your room, just ask for one by saying **Minta térmos air panas**. Better hotels will have complimentary sachets of tea, coffee and sugar, and possibly also a small fridge.

Transportation
There is a variety of public transportation in Indonesia, some forms quaint, some increasingly modern. Shorter distances can be covered by vehicles such as Jakarta's **bajaj** (like the Thai *tuktuk*), and outside Jakarta, by rickshaws or **bécak** and **ojék** (motorcycle taxi). These require some bargaining.

Flat rates operate on public buses and minibuses (**angkot** or **angkutan kota**) as well as trains. Mini-buses can be flagged down anywhere. However, taxis are your safest bet. Ask for one with a meter. Blue Bird is the best known company.

▶ How can I get there?
  Naik apa ke sana?

▶ Do you know the way to ... ?
  Apa tahu jalan ke ... ?

▶ How much should it cost to go to ... ?
  Kira-kira berapa kalau ke ... ?

▶ Can I walk there?
  Bisa jalan kaki?

▶ Can you call me a taxi / rickshaw?
  Bisa dipanggil taksi / bécak?

▶ How much is the rate for a taxi into town?
  Berapa ongkos taksi ke kota?

▶ Is it a metered taxi?
  Apa itu taksi argo atau bukan?

▶ Can you please take me to ... ?
  Tolong antarkan saya ke ... ?

▶ Could you please wait here for a little while?
Tolong ditunggu sebentar.

▶ I will come back.
Sebentar lagi saya kembali.

▶ Can I order a taxi?
Boléh pesan taksi?

▶ A cheap taxi is fine.
Taksi murah juga boléh.

▶ I want a taxi from a respectable company.
Saya mau taksi dari perusahaan yang baik.

▶ Can you change a Rp.100,000 note?
Bisa ditukar uang seratus ribu?

▶ Keep the change.
Kembalinya tidak usah.

▶ How much is it to ... ?
Kalau ke ..., berapa ya?

▶ Can you go any cheaper?
Bisa kurang?

▶ Where is this bus / minibus going?
Apa jurusannya bis / angkot ini?

▶ I want the bus / minibus for ... .
Saya mau bis / angkot jurusan ... .

▶ Stop!
Kiri!

▶ I want to get off.
Saya mau turun.

Directions

left	**kiri**
right	**kanan**
straight ahead	**terus, lurus**
stop	**berhenti, setop**
north	**utara**
south	**selatan**
east	**timur**
west	**barat**
here	**di sini**
there	**di sana**
in front	**di depan**
behind	**di belakang**
beside	**di samping, di sebelah**
opposite	**di seberang**
turn	**bélok**
turn around, do a U-turn	**putar balik**

▶ How do I get to ... ?
  Bagaimana saya ke ... ?

by taxi	**naik taksi**
by rickshaw	**naik bécak**
by motorcycle	**naik ojék**
by foot	**jalan kaki**
by *tuktuk*	**naik bajaj** [say *bajai*]
by train	**naik keréta (api)**
by bus	**naik bis**
by horse and cart	**naik délman / andong / béndi / sado**
	[words differ locally]

▶ Turn left up ahead.
  Di depan bélok kiri.

▶ Take the first left turn.
  Di simpang pertama bélok kiri.

▶ Turn around / do a U-turn.
  Putar balik.

via the park	**léwat taman**
on the toll road (usually quicker)	**léwat jalan tol**

▶ Please slow down!
  Tolong jangan ngebut!

▶ Please drive carefully.
  Tolong hati-hati.

Increasingly, long-distance travel is made by air, thanks to cheaper tickets. The train system in Java and Sumatra continues to improve and is a scenic alternative. Inter-provincial buses are perhaps the cheapest (but not necessarily most pleasant) way to travel long distances. Between large cities which are relatively close (e.g. Bandung-Jakarta, Surabaya-Malang) there may be cheap and frequent shuttle buses called **travél**.

station	**setasiun**
platform	**péron**
train	**keréta api, keréta**
carriage	**gerbong**
economy class	**kelas ékonomi**
business class (usually cheap)	**kelas bisnis**
executive class (usually with air-con)	**kelas éksékutif**
arrive	**datang**
depart	**berangkat**
timetable	**jadwal**

ticket	**tikét, karcis**
adult fare	**karcis déwasa**
child's fare	**karcis anak**
seat	**tempat duduk**
window seat	**tempat duduk di jendéla**
aisle seat	**tempat duduk di lorong**
dining car	**gerbong restorasi**
air-conditioning	**AC** [say *ah-se*]
fan	**kipas angin**
destination	**jurusan**
bus terminal	**términal bis**

▶ Where is the station?
   Di mana setasiun?

▶ I want to buy a ticket to ...
   Saya mau ke ...

▶ Two adults and one child.
   Dua déwasa dan satu anak.

▶ What time does the train leave?
   Jam berapa kerétanya berangkat?

▶ How much is the total cost?
   Berapa semuanya?

▶ Does it stop at ... ?
   Apakah berhenti di ...?

▶ Which platform does it leave from?
   Berangkat dari péron berapa?

▶ Could we please sit together?
   Kami minta duduk bersama.

▶ Could I please have a window seat?
   Minta tempat duduk di jendéla.

▶ Can you buy food on the bus / train?
   Apa bisa beli makanan di keréta api / bis?

▶ Is there air-con or a fan?
   Apa ada AC [say *ah-se*] **atau kipas angin saja?**

▶ When is the next stop?
   Kapan berhenti lagi?

▶ Where is the next stop?
   Di mana berhenti nanti?

▶ I've lost my ticket.
   Tikét saya hilang.

▶ I think someone is sitting in my seat.
  Sepertinya ada yang duduk di tempat saya.

▶ Can I bring my bike on board?
  Boléh bawa sepéda?

▶ Where can I put my baggage?
  Bagasi bisa taruh di mana?

You may need to buy an entrance ticket to the bus
terminal, or platform ticket at a station. Beware of
pickpockets and anyone who tries to sell you a ticket
other than at the official ticket counter.

EXPLORING THE TOWN

bank	**bank**
bus terminal	**términal (bis)**
cathedral	**katédral**
church	**geréja**
cinema	**bioskop**
hotel	**hotél**
language school	**sekolah bahasa, kursus bahasa**
mall / shopping centre	**mal / pusat perbelanjaan**
market	**pasar**
mosque	**mesjid**

museum	**musium**
park	**taman**
post office	**kantor pos**
restaurant	**réstoran, rumah makan**
river	**sungai, kali**
school	**sekolah**
elementary school	**SD** [*es-de*]
junior high school	**SMP** [*es-em-pe*]
senior high school	**SMA** [*es-em-ah*]
shop	**toko**
shopping district	**pertokoan**
station	**setasiun**
Chinese temple	**klénténg, kuil, pagoda**
Balinese temple	**pura**
Hindu or Buddhist temple	**candi, kuil**
theater	**téater**
toilet	**toilét, WC umum**
tourist information office	**kantor pariwisa**
town square	**alun-alun, lapangan**
town hall	**balaikota**
university	**kampus, univérsitas**
beautiful	**bagus sekali**
old	**lama**
new	**baru**
historic	**bersejarah**
modern	**modérn, baru**

big	**besar**
small	**kecil**
in Dutch times	**jaman Belanda**

▶ What year was it built?
  Dibangun tahun berapa?

▶ It was built in 1820.
  Dibangun tahun 1820 (delapan belas dua puluh).

▶ Do you have a map of the town?
  Ada peta kota?

▶ What time does it open?
  Jam berapa bukanya?

▶ It opens at 10 a.m.
  Buka jam 10 (sepuluh) pagi.

▶ How much is the entrance fee?
  Berapa biaya masuk?

▶ (The entrance fee is) Rp.10,000.
  (Biaya masuk) Rp.10.000 (sepuluh ribu rupiah).

The best way to explore most towns is on foot,
with a map only as a back-up. Maps in Indonesia
have a habit of being out-of-date, inaccurate or

or misleading – including online ones. Larger towns may have a small tourist information office. These can be very helpful and may have information about tours or guides.

Road signs

Children	**anak-anak**
You are entering a minimum-3-passenger zone	**Anda memasuki kawasan three-in-one**
Winds from the side (on bridges)	**Angin dari samping**
Look out	**Awas**
Airport	**Bandara**
Pay with exact money	**Bayar uang pas**
Turn left	**Belok kiri**
Turn right	**Belok kanan**
Stop	**Berhenti**
Roundabout, traffic circle	**Bundaran**
No entry	**Dilarang masuk**
Two-way traffic	**Dua arah**
Be careful	**Hati-hati**
Dead-end	**Jalan buntu**
Flyover	**Jalan layang**
Slippery when wet	**Jalan licin**
Toll road	**Jalan tol**
Bridge	**Jembatan**
Pedestrian overpass	**Jembatan penyeberangan**

Exit	**Keluar**
No entry to three-wheeled motor vehicles	**Kendaraan bermotor roda tiga dilarang masuk**
Turn left at any time	**Kiri langsung**
City, town	**Kota**
Green light	**Lampu hijau**
Amber light, yellow light	**Lampu kuning**
Red light	**Lampu mérah**
Traffic	**Lalu lintas**
Entry	**Masuk**
Angle parking	**Parkir sérong**
Railway crossing	**Penyeberangan keréta api**
Roadworks	**Perbaikan jalan**
Automatic gate	**Pintu otomatis**
One way	**Satu arah**
School	**Sekolah**
Tunnel, underpass	**Terowongan**

> The abundance of cheap, local drivers who know the way to all the good tourist spots means that you are unlikely to do any driving yourself in a hired car, unless you particularly want to. Driving yourself also runs the risk of not knowing local traffic regulations, which can become a problem when your appearance is obviously foreign.

Shopping

Indonesia generally offers very good value for money

in terms of shopping. While you can bargain in markets and smaller establishments, shops in malls and big cities usually have fixed prices—unless the assistant says those magic words, **boléh kurang** (lit. discount allowed) or **boléh ditawar** (lit. bargaining allowed).

shopping district	**pertokoan**
mall/shopping centre	**mal / pusat perbelanjaan**
shophouses	**ruko (rumah toko)**
roadside stall	**warung, kedai** (in Sumatra)
jewelers	**toko emas**
bookshop	**toko buku**
toyshop	**mainan**
pharmacy, chemist	**apotik, apoték**
clothes shop	**toko baju**
electronics store	**toko éléktronik**
shoe shop	**toko sepatu**
laundry (usually for upmarket items)	**binatu, waserai**
haberdashery	**toko kain**
bakery	**toko roti**
bike shop	**toko sepéda**
garage, workshop	**béngkél**

Traditionally, Indonesian shops lined the main street of the town, with owners often living either behind or above the shop. In modern times, this continues with the development of **ruko** (shophouses), which follow the Chinese practice of living above your shop.

There are no greengrocers or butchers as such; these items would be found either at the local market (**pasar**) or more expensive supermarket (**pasar swalayan**). News agencies are unknown; buy your newspapers or magazines from displays in supermarkets, stations and other public places; on the side of the road; or from itinerant sellers. Flowers are best bought from markets or small stalls near cemeteries as florists are not only expensive but few and far between. Indonesians usually only give flowers on a congratulatory occasion, or if someone has been quite unwell.

Warung (Roadside foodstalls)

The local neighborhood **warung** sells small cooking and household items (such as butter, cleaning supplies, sweets, eggs, etc.). **Warung** are increasingly being sidelined by chains of minimarkets. If you want to support a local family or small business, shop at the **warung**.

Warung is also the term for a roadside stall selling ready-cooked food. There may be whole districts devoted to these cheap and often tasty eateries. Do be careful with hygiene, however, as many **warung** do not have access to running water and may be washing vegetables, plates or cutlery in less than clean water.

Warkop stands for **warung kopi**, a local café (authentically Indonesian long before the invasion of international chains).

Warteg is short for **warung Tegal**, which are super-cheap eateries specializing in simple fare such as fried eggs, tofu, *tempe* and rice. Tegal is a city in Central Java where many of the owners / sellers come from.

Warnét (warung internét) are a good place to check your email or surf the net. Many school children without computers at home also use them for gaming.

Wartél or **warung télékomunikasi** once ruled the cables but are now rare as mobile phone coverage intensifies. You can call local, long-distance or over-seas, and send faxes.

local	**lokal**
long-distance	**interlokal, SLJJ** *(sambung-an langsung jarak jauh)*
international	**internasional, SLI** *(sam-bungan langsung internasi-onal)*

Warpostél also provide postal services.

Markets
In many towns, and even suburbs of large cities, the market is the focal point of life. It is also probably the cheapest and often the only place to buy vegetables, fruit, cheap food and various items such as raincoats, gumboots, etc.

▶ How much is this?
  Berapa harganya?

▶ Can we bargain?
  Boléh ditawar?

▶ Yes (lit. allowed).
  Boléh.

▶ No (lit. fixed price).
  Tidak, harga pas.

▶ What about [price]?
  Kalau [harga], bagaimana ya?

▶ Rp.20.000.
  Dua puluh ribu rupiah. (often shortened to **dua puluh ribu** or **just dua puluh**)

▶ That's expensive.
  Mahal ya ... .

▶ I'm looking for something (more) ... .
  Saya cari yang lebih ... .

larger	**besar**
smaller	**kecil**
cheaper	**murah**
better	**bagus**

▶ Do you have any ... ?
Ada yang ... ?

more ... / ...-er	**lebih ...**
in blue	**warna biru**

▶ I'll come back later.
Nanti saya kembali.

▶ I'll take five (of these).
Saya mau ambil lima.

five (general counter)	**lima buah**
five (for small items)	**lima biji**
five (pairs)	**lima pasang** (shoes, but not trousers or glasses)
free of charge	**gratis**

Refer to page 25 for more details on counters.

▶ I'm looking for ... .
Saya mencari ... .

fruit and vegetables	**sayur-sayuran dan buah-buahan**
meat	**daging** (arguably more hygienic if bought at a supermarket)

nuts	**kacang-kacangan**
the toilet	**kamar kecil / WC** [say *weh-seh*]
clothes	**baju / pakaian**
batik	**batik**
handicrafts	**kerajinan**
the stairs	**tangga**
the ground floor	**lantai dasar / lantai bawah**
the entrance	**pintu masuk**
the exit	**pintu keluar**

Some markets are a tourist destination in themselves, such as Pasar Kléwér (the batik market in Solo), Pasar Beringharjo in Yogyakarta or Pasar Mayéstik in Jakarta. In the capital, Mangga Dua and Tanah Abang are also urban versions specializing in clothing (and electronics) at wholesale prices. Enjoy these very lively, dynamic places, but be careful with your wallet, as pickpockets abound.

In traditional markets and modes of transport, bargaining is the norm. For people who are unfamiliar with bargaining, this can be uncomfortable and a little confronting. It's actually all a game! The sellers will not be offended if you don't buy, and they expect (and enjoy) banter over the price. You should also avoid trying to beat them down to the lowest possible price—while foreigners are often overcharged, on the other side of the coin, remember that you do usually have greater purchasing power than locals. For good deals on pricier items, feign disinterest and even take a step or two away. Soon you will enjoy bargaining and be picking up good value purchases.

AT THE MALL

In larger cities, and increasingly in smaller towns across the archipelago, shopping malls are popping up everywhere. In big cities these often boast international brands and are a good source of (usually) clean public toilets.

Typical shops at the mall might include most of the above, plus the following:

ATM	**ATM** [say *ah-te-em*]
bank	**bank**
basement	**bésmén**
café	**kafé**
carpark	**tempat parkir, parkiran**
children's indoor playground	**tempat bermain anak-anak**
cinema	**bioskop**
department store	**tosérba (toko sérba ada)**
elevator	**lift**
escalator	**éskalator**

fast food restaurants	**réstoran cepat saji, réstoran siap saji**
floor, level, story	**lantai**
money changer	**jasa tukar uang**
salon	**potong rambut, salon**
supermarkets	**swalayan, supermarkét**
taxi stand	**pangkalan taksi**

▶ Where is the money changer?
  Bisa tukar uang di mana?

▶ On the third floor.
  Di lantai tiga.

▶ What time do you open?
  Jam berapa buka?

▶ What time do you close?
  Jam berapa tutup?

Mall culture has well and truly arrived in Indonesia. The concept of spending a morning or afternoon at an air-conditioned mall, either window-shopping or spending up big, is enticing for many Indonesians.

There is some confusion about terms for the ground floor of malls and indeed tall buildings in general. Some buildings will refer to this as **lantai dasar** (lit. ground floor) while others will call it

lantai satu (first floor). If in doubt use **lantai dasar**. The first floor up is probably most safely called **lantai dua**. (So you could have a building where there is no official **lantai satu**!)

As well as being department stores, **tosérba (toko sérba ada)** can also be small supermarkets, usually quite cheap. **Pasar swalayan** (or just **swalayan**) is the local word for supermarkets, although **supermarkét** is often heard. The larger supermarkets such as Superindo, Hero and international chains like Carrefour or Giant stock many staples of Western food such as bread, and are one of the few places you can get fresh milk outside big cities.

Groceries

Most large towns have a supermarket (Hero, Griya, Superindo are some common ones), while minimarkets are ubiquitous nowadays, even in remote places. Some items you may want that can be found in supermarkets, and many minimarkets, include:

biscuits	**kué kering**
bread	**roti**
cheese	**kéju**
chocolate	**cokelat**
cup noodles	**pop mie, mi gelas**
drinking water	**air minum**
fruit	**buah-buahan**

insect repellent	**obat nyamuk**
milk	**susu**
moisturiser	**pelembab**
mosquito coils	**koil anti nyamuk**
pens	**bolpoin, péna**
sanitary pads	**pembalut**
soap	**sabun**
sunblock	**krim tabur surya**
sweets	**permén**
toilet paper	**tisu gulung**
writing paper	**kertas tulis**

For the following supermarket items you may be better off buying in small, portable quantities at the local **warung** where you can buy by the sachet.

conditioner	**pelembab rambut, kondisioner**
shampoo	**sampo**
tissues	**tisu**
washing powder	**sabun cuci baju**

On the other hand, big cities may offer international standard supermarkets such as Carrefour, Ranch Market, or Sogo, to name a few, if you are hunkering for foreign food unavailable elsewhere. Obviously prices are much dearer.

cereal	**séréal**
cheese	**kéju**
instant pasta	**pasta instan**
pork	**daging babi**
sausages	**sosis**
sushi	**sushi**
wine	**anggur**
yoghurt	**yogurt**

Souvenirs

One of the charms about Indonesia is how handicrafts vary from region to region. Try to buy gifts which are handmade, and appreciate that the price tag may not be the amount that the original artisan actually earned.

▶ How much does this cost?
  Berapa harganya?

▶ Where was this made?
  Ini buatan mana?

▶ Did you make this yourself?
  Apa ini dibuat sendiri?

▶ It's really nice.
  Bagus sekali.

▶ Do you have it in another color?
  Ada warna lain?

▶ Thanks, I might come back.
  Terima kasih, mungkin nanti saya kembali.

Items found across Indonesia include:

bags	**tas**
batik	**batik**
bracelets, bangles	**gelang**
carvings	**ukiran**
earrings	**anting, giwang**
embroidery	**sulaman**
fans	**kipas**
gemstones	**batu mulia**
jewelry	**perhiasan**
leather	**kulit**
puppets	**wayang**
rings	**cincin**
necklaces	**kalung**
paintings	**lukisan**
shells	**kerang**
silverware	**kerajinan pérak**
weavings	**ikat, tenunan**

And of course generic souvenirs such as

dolls	**bonéka**
fridge magnets	**magnét**
keyrings	**gantungan kunci**
wallets	**dompét**

Long-lasting food items can also be good souvenirs. Be aware that depending on your country of origin, you may have to declare food at customs when returning home, or indeed other items made from wood, leaves and natural products.

chocolate	**cokelat**
coffee	**kopi**
crisps, chips	**keripik**
honey	**madu**
jelly sweets	**agar-agar**
nuts	**kacang, kacang-kacangan**
tea	**téh**

Indonesia has an amazing array of souvenirs for all tastes. Whether you want cute, elegant, tacky or just so ostentatious that you have to buy it, there will be something for you. The culture of bringing **oléh-oléh** (souvenirs) back home for friends and family after a trip is very strong. By doing so, you will both assist the local economy and promote Indonesia among your family and friends.

Books and other reading material

▶ Do you sell English <u>books</u>?
Apa bisa beli <u>buku</u> berbahasa Inggris di sini?

guidebooks	**buku panduan wisata**
magazines	**majalah**
maps	**peta**
newspapers	**koran, surat kabar**

▶ I am looking for a <u>guidebook</u>.
Saya mencari <u>buku panduan wisata</u>.

children's book	**buku anak-anak**
cookbook	**buku résép memasak**
dictionary	**kamus**
novel	**novél, roman**
phrasebook	**buku ungkapan, buku frasa**
translation	**terjemahan**

▶ I am looking for books <u>in English</u>.
Saya mencari buku <u>dalam bahasa Inggris</u>.

| in Mandarin | **dalam bahasa Mandarin** |
| in Javanese | **dalam bahasa Jawa** |

▶ Do you have a copy in newer condition?
Apa ada yang baru?

▶ I am looking for a book by ...
   Saya mencari buku karya ...

> While there is not a huge variety of English-language
> reading material available throughout the archipela-
> go, in large cities (especially in Java) this has become
> much more widely available as part of the English-
> language education boom among the middle and
> upper classes. Large, glitzy shopping malls nearly
> always have a bookshop. The *Jakarta Post* and the
> *Jakarta Globe* are both English-language daily news-
> papers; the well-respected current affairs magazine
> *Tempo* also publishes an English-language version.
> Imported magazines are available in airports, inter-
> national supermarkets and bookshops like Gramédia
> and Periplus.

Clothing

clothes	**pakaian, baju**
clothes shop	**toko pakaian, toko baju**

▶ I would like to buy a <u>skirt</u>.
   Saya mencari <u>rok</u>.

belt	**ikat pinggang**
bra	**béha, kutang**
dress	**rok (panjang)**
hat, cap	**topi**

jeans	**celana jins**
kebaya (traditional Indonesian blouse)	**kebaya**
pair of trousers	**celana**
sarong	**sarung**
scarf, shawl	**seléndang**
singlet	**baju singlét, baju dalam**
shirt (with collar)	**keméja** (men), **blus** (women)
shorts	**celana péndék**
socks	**kaus kaki**
sunglasses	**kacamata hitam**
T-shirt	**kaus**
underpants	**celana dalam**
with sleeves	**berléngan**
with long sleeves	**berléngan panjang**
sleeveless	**tidak berléngan**

▶ It fits well; I'll take it.
Pas, saya ambil.

▶ It's too tight.
Terlalu sempit.

▶ Do you have a larger / smaller size?
Apa ada ukuran lebih besar / kecil?

▶ Do you have it in a different color?
  Apa ada warna lain?

For some reason, cotton clothing is not always easily
available in Indonesia, and often costs more than the
ubiquitous polyester.

cotton	**katun**
denim	**(bahan) jins**
polyester	**poli, sintétis**
silk	**sutera**

Footwear

Footwear in Indonesia is a little more formal than you
might expect. Thongs and flipflops are generally worn
inside the house, or for wandering out to the **warung**
and back. For a trip to the mall or out for dinner, it is
better to wear proper sandals. All footwear is taken off
before entering someone's home (regardless of religion)
and mosques.

clogs	**kelom; bakiak** (traditional)
high heels	**sepatu hak tinggi**
rubber boots, gumboots, Wellingtons	**sepatu karét**
sandals	**sepatu sendal**
shoes	**sepatu**
slippers	**selop**

sports shoes	**sepatu kéts**
thongs / flipflops	**sendal jepit**

> Clothing for every type of budget is available. Obviously cheap and cheerful pants from the market or souvenir stall are not likely to last as long as branded jeans from a foreign chain store at a Jakarta mall, but they may well be more comfortable in the tropical climate, and easier to wash and dry.
>
> Remember to dress modestly. You may find the heat exhausting, or be enjoying your holiday, but do not wear anything out in public that you would not wear in your hometown. Strappy tops, very short shorts and large areas of exposed skin are asking for unwanted attention, as well as being possibly offensive to locals.

SIGHTSEEING

▶ What is there to visit around here?
Ada obyék wisata apa di daérah ini?

▶ How do I get there?
Bagaimana bisa ke sana?

▶ Can I get a tour?
Bisa ikut tur?

▶ How long is the tour?
Turnya berapa lama?

▶ Is there a guide?
Apa ada pemandu wisata?

▶ How much should I pay the guide?
Biaya pemandu wisata berapa?

▶ Does the guide speak English?
Apa ada pemandu wisata berbahasa Inggris?

▶ There is a / an ...
Ada ...

art gallery	**galéri seni**
batik studio	**studio batik**
botanic gardens	**kebun raya**
cinema	**bioskop**
exhibition hall	**tempat paméran**
factory	**pabrik**
historic building	**gedung bersejarah**
jail	**penjara**
library	**perpustakaan**
monument	**monumén**
museum	**musium**
natural attractions	**wisata alam**
nightlife	**kehidupan malam**

palace	**istana**
restaurants	**wisata kulinér**
scenic view	**pemandangan**
school	**sekolah**
souvenir shop	**toko cenderamata**
temple	**candi / kuil / klénténg / pura**
theater	**téater**
tourist information center	**kantor pariwisata**
travel agent	**agén perjalanan**
tunnels (Dutch or Japanese)	**gua Belanda, gua Jepang**
zoo	**kebun binatang (bonbin)**

▶ It's ... rupiah per hour.
  ... rupiah per jam.

There are so-called "tourist objects" (**obyék wisata**) dotted around Indonesia, which consist of genuinely interesting places, as well as what locals deem to be of interest to visitors. This means that an artificial replica of someone turned to stone in a local legend might be considered worthy of being included on tours, along with stops at honestly breathtaking views. In particular, houses once inhabited by national heroes, tunnels dug during the war by the Japanese or Dutch, local government buildings and monuments (usually pillars) are proudly promoted as **obyék wisa-ta**—and some are indeed well worth a visit.

Museums

▶ How much is the entrance ticket?
  Berapa karcis masuk?

▶ What time does it open?
  Jam berapa buka?

▶ What time does it close?
  Jam berapa tutup?

▶ What days is it open?
  Hari apa saja buka?

▶ Is there a guidebook?
  Ada buku panduan?

Many museums may offer you a guide. This could be a good way of meeting a local, getting information about displays and being able to ask questions.

▶ Do you have guides?
  Ada pemandu?

▶ Where does this come from?
  Ini berasal dari mana?

▶ What year is this?
Ini dari tahun berapa ya?

▶ Who is this?
Siapa itu?

▶ What's this for?
Ini untuk apa?

▶ It's lovely.
Bagus ya.

▶ It's really interesting.
Menarik sekali.

▶ I want to see the ...
Saya ingin melihat ...

batik	**batik**
palace heirlooms	**pusaka istana**
pottery	**tembikar, keramik**
maps	**peta**
jewelry	**perhiasan**
clothes	**busana, baju**
weavings	**ikat, tenunan**
king / queen	**raja / ratu**
prince / princess	**pangeran / permaisuri**
kingdom	**kerajaan**

sultan / sultanate	**sultan / kesultanan**
resident / residency	**résidén / karésidénan**
regent / regency	**bupati / kabupatén**
government	**pemerintah**
Dutch East India company (VOC)	**Kompéni**
Dutch, Netherlands	**Belanda**
Portuguese, Portugal	**Portugis**
Malay	**Melayu**
Chinese, China	**Cina / Tiongkok**
Japanese, Japan	**Jepang**
English, England	**Inggris**
Javanese, Java	**Jawa**
Sundanese	**Sunda**
Buginese	**Bugis**
capital (city)	**ibukota**
war	**perang**
to occupy, colonize	**menjajah**
occupation, colonization	**penjajahan**
jail, prison	**penjara**
hero	**pahlawan**

Indonesia's generally lower standard of living has resulted in many museums being underfunded and in a poor state of upkeep. The very low entrance prices may contribute to this! Luckily, awareness of the importance of museums to national pride (as well as the more lucrative tourism industry) is slowly growing. Remember to focus on the artefacts themselves rather than dowdy display cases or labels in poor English.

Some recommended museums include the Muséum Géologi in Bandung, which has great, relatively modern displays of both dinosaurs and volcanoes, the Musium Tsunami in Banda Aceh, and the Sampoerna Museum in Surabaya.

Toilets

▶ Where is the toilet?
   Di mana kamar kecil? / WC? [*we-se*] **/ toilét?**

ladies	**wanita**
gents	**pria**
urinating ("no. 1s")	**buang air kecil / kencing**
defecating ("no. 2s")	**buang air besar**
washing	**mandi**

▶ There's no water.
   Tidak ada air.

▶ The tap is broken.
   Kerannya rusak.

▶ It won't flush.
   Tidak bisa disiram.

toilet paper	**tisu gulung**
dipper	**gayung**

It is good to be prepared for Indonesian toilets. They are usually spotless in posh malls or hotels, but may decline in comfort and cleanliness the further you stray from the modern world. While sit-down toilets are widespread, they may not always flush, which will require you to do this "manually" with a dipper from the ever-present bucket or **bak** (tub) of water. (A few well-directed streams from on high should do the trick.) This is also how to flush squat toilets.

Many toilets, especially the less clean ones, require a payment of Rp.1.000 or 2.000 per person per visit. This can be exasperating if the toilet is filthy, but is deserved if the money is helping to keep the toilet clean. There may or may not be someone guarding the box for payment.

Toilet paper is rarely available outside Western haunts, Indonesians preferring to use water to clean themselves. If you find this a little damp, you may want to keep a small supply of tissues with you at all times. Used toilet paper should NOT be flushed away, but put in a bin, which is usually provided.

On the road, there are almost always decent toilets at gas stations. Look for the Pertamina sign denoting Indonesia's state oil company.

EATING OUT

Indonesia is a foodie's paradise. There are restaurants of all shapes and sizes, from high society haunts to roadside stalls—with the best food not necessarily being found in the most salubrious establishments. Use discretion when choosing where to eat. Does the place look clean? Does the menu seem reasonably priced? A very good indicator is if the restaurant looks busy. If the locals are eating there, then it's probably a good place for you to eat, too.

Food

▶ What kind of food do you have?
   Ada makanan apa di sini?

Indonesian food	**Makanan Indonésia**
Javanese food	**Makanan Jawa**
Western food	**Makanan Barat**
Japanese	**Jepang**
Italian	**Itali**
Chinese	**Cina / Tiongkok**
vegetarian	**végétarian**

▶ Do you have ... food?
   Apa ada masakan ... ?

▶ I want a table for ... .
Kami ber .... . (number)

| two | **berdua** |
| five | **berlima** |

▶ I would like ... .
Minta ... .

white rice	**nasi putih**
fried rice	**nasi goréng**
vegetables	**sayur**
meat	**daging**

Chinese restaurants tend to offer seafood and varieties of noodles. If you are longing for pork then you are more likely to find it here than anywhere else. They are also more likely to understand requests for vegetarian food.

▶ I am vegetarian. I don't eat meat.
Saya végétarian. Saya tidak makan daging.

▶ I don't eat ... .
Saya tidak makan ... .

pork	**daging babi**
fish	**ikan**
beef	**daging sapi**
seafood	**makanan laut/seafood**

▶ I only eat vegetables.
  Saya hanya makan sayur.

sweet	**manis**
sour	**asam**
salty	**asin**
bitter	**pahit**
eat here	**makan di sini**
takeaway	**dibungkus**

▶ Can I please have this wrapped up to take home?
  Minta bungkus.

▶ Could we please have separate bills?
  Minta *bill*-nya dipisah.

If they are still uncertain, you can add:

▶ **Kami mau bayar masing-masing** (we want to pay
  individually).

Indonesian restaurants serve white rice, to be eaten
with two or three side-dishes (**lauk-pauk**). Fried rice
(**nasi goréng**) is generally a meal on its own. Side-
dishes may include vegetables, meat, soup, eggs, tofu
and *tempe* (fried unprocessed bean-curd).
   If there is heaps of food left over, you may want
to ask for it to be wrapped up and taken home. This

is very common across Indonesia and not at all cheapskate. You can even order food at a **warung** or restaurant to take home, rather than be eaten then and now. All you have to say is **minta bungkus**.

Food in Indonesia is usually eaten together, often with those at the same table ordering dishes to share rather than individual orders. Similarly, the concept of each diner paying for their own food is still foreign, even in big cities. Some restaurants actually refuse to write up separate bills. It is often easier for one diner to pay, then sort out who owes what, but if you insist on separate bills, say **Minta bill-nya dipisah**.

Drink

Generally, patrons will also order a drink to stay hydrated, usually something cold to go with the meal, possibly before a warmer beverage later. Fruit juices are delicious although you may want to skip the ice in smaller roadside eateries. If you want ice, you can replace the word **jus** with **es** (i.e. **jus strobéri** becomes **és strobéri**). Some of these are almost a meal in their own right—especially **air kelapa**, as the young coconut meat fills you up and makes a perfect dessert.

juice	**jus / sari buah**
with milk	**pakai susu**
avocado	**alpukat**

banana	**pisang**
carrot	**wortel**
strawberry	**strobéri**
orange	**jeruk**
soursop	**sirsak**
cucumber	**timun / mentimun**
watermelon	**semangka**
with ice	**pakai és**
no ice	**tidak pakai és / tanpa és**
tea	**téh**
coffee	**kopi**
with sugar	**pakai gula**
with milk	**pakai susu**

Tea is never drunk with milk (except for the Malay import of **téh tarik**.) In Central and East Java, it is always sweet; ask for no sugar if you prefer. In West Java tea is usually unsweetened.

Coffee can either come out of a packet or you can try the traditional **kopi tubruk**, where you wait for the dregs to sink before sipping it as it cools down. **Kopi tubruk** can also be drunk with condensed milk. In coffee-producing areas like Aceh, you should forgo cheap instant alternatives and instead treat yourself to a proper, delicious fresh coffee at a **warung kopi**.

In traditional restaurants, tea is usually provided free, as something to drink before your meal arrives.

MONEY

All money of any value is in the thousands denomination, which makes the word **ribu** a compulsory prefix to the word **rupiah**, the name for the national currency.

Rp.1.000 **seribu rupiah**   worth a trip to the toilet
blue-green banknote
These notes are being phased out by shiny new
Rp.1.000 coins.

Rp.2.000 **dua ribu rupiah**   worth a ride on a minibus
gray banknote

Rp.5.000 **lima ribu rupiah**   worth a bottle of drink-
cream-colored banknote   ing water

Rp.10.000 **sepuluh ribu**   worth a couple of buns
    rupiah
purple banknote

Rp.20.000 **dua puluh ribu**   worth a *becak* ride
    rupiah
green banknote

Rp.50.000 **lima piluh ribu**   worth lunch in a food
    rupiah   court
blue banknote

Rp.100.000 **seratus ribu rupiah**
red banknote

worth two weeks' mobile phone credit

In terms of coins, Rp.500, Rp.200 and Rp.100 pieces still exist; these are used mainly for paying public transport fares or for giving to buskers or the poor.

Rp.100 **seratus rupiah**
small silver coin

worth dropping in a donation box

Rp.200 **dua ratus rupiah**
slightly larger and thicker silver coin

worth a sweet

Rp.500 **lima ratus rupiah**
larger silver or gold coin

useful on public transport

Rp.1.000 **seribu rupiah**
small, shiny silver coin

often given as change in shops

▶ I want to change money.
   Saya mau tukar uang.

▶ What is your rate?
   Berapa kursnya?

▶ What is your rate for US dollars?
   Berapa kursnya untuk dolar Amérika?

▶ That's a bit expensive.
   Sedikit mahal, ya.

▶ OK, I'll change one hundred US dollars.
   Baik, saya tukar seratus dolar Amérika.

▶ Do you have an envelope?
   Boléh minta amplop?

▶ Until what time are you open?
   Buka sampai jam berapa?

Australian dollar	**dolar Australia** (sometimes **Ustralia** or **Ustrali**)
Canadian dollar	**dolar Kanada**
euros	**euro**
Hong Kong dollar	**dolar Hong Kong**
Korean won	**won**
ringgit	**ringgit**
New Zealand dollar	**dolar Selandia Baru**
pésos	**péso**
rials	**rial**
roubles	**rubel**
Singapore dollar	**dolar Singapura**
rand	**rand**

UK pound sterling	**pon stérling**
US dollar	**dolar Amérika, dolar AS**
	(*ah es*)
yen	**yén**
yuan	**yuan**
buying	**membeli**
selling	**menjual**

> There are plenty of money changers, official and
> unofficial, in tourist areas and shopping malls. Shop
> around for a good rate. It is definitely better to change
> your money in Indonesia, as overseas rates for *rupiah*
> are poor. ATMs are often a practical way to access
> your bank account at home and receive cash in *rupiah*
> (although obviously there is an inter-bank fee).

MEASUREMENTS

millimeter	**mili, miliméter** (mm)
centimeter	**sénti, séntiméter** (cm)
meter	**méter** (m)
kilometer	**kilométer** (km)
square centimeter	**séntiméter persegi**
square meter	**méter persegi**
hectare	**héktar**
inch	**inci**
foot	**kaki**

yard	**tiga kaki**
mile	**mil**
cubic centimeter	**cc** [say *se se*]
cubic meter	**méter kubik**
liter	**liter** (L)
gallon	**galon**
milligram	**miligram** (mg)
gram	**gram** (g)
kilogram	**kilo** (kg)
tonne	**ton** (T)
ounce	**ons**

Indonesia uses the metric system of weights and measurements. While a few imperial measurement units are known, they are not common. Exceptions include ounces (for cooking).

TIME

Saying the time is very logical, by adding a number after the word **jam** to give you the hour. You can then add on minutes (**menit**) or quarters as you wish.

one o'clock	**jam satu**
two o'clock	**jam dua**
two o'clock in the afternoon	**jam dua <u>siang</u>**

morning	**pagi**
middle of the day	**siang**
late afternoon / evening	**soré**
night	**malam**
a quarter past one	**jam satu (léwat) seperempat**
a quarter to two	**jam dua kurang seperempat**
half past one	**jam setengah dua**
one fifteen	**jam satu léwat limabelas (menit)**
one twenty	**jam satu léwat dua puluh**

▶ What time is it?
   Jam berapa sekarang?

▶ It's eleven o'clock.
   Jam sebelas.

eleven o'clock in the morning	**jam sebelas siang**
eleven o'clock in the evening	**jam sebelas malam**

▶ How long will it take?
   (Makan waktu) berapa lama?

two hours	**dua jam**
approximately	**kira-kira, sekitar**

▶ What time do we / does it arrive?
  Jam berapa tiba / sampai?

▶ What time do we / does it leave?
  Jam berapa berangkat?

> The only slightly tricky concept is that of half past
> the hour. In Indonesian, we say "half to" the next
> hour (as in some European languages such as Dutch).
> Basically, half past and beyond will refer to the fol-
> lowing hour in Indonesian.
>   Be aware that for official times and schedules,
> Indonesia uses the 24-hour clock. Confusingly, people
> often translate 24-hour time into everyday hours. So
> while an official might announce the time as **jam dela-
> pan belas** (18.00), a passenger might tell her friend that
> the time is **jam enam soré** (6.00 in the evening).

DAYS OF THE WEEK

Monday	**hari Senin**
	(sometimes **Senén**)
Tuesday	**hari Selasa**
Wednesday	**hari Rabu**
	(sometimes **Rebo**)
Thursday	**hari Kamis**
	(sometimes **Kemis**)

Friday	**hari Jumat**
Saturday	**hari Sabtu**
Sunday	**hari Minggu** (occasionally **Ahad** in Islamic areas)

the day before yesterday	**kemarin dulu**
yesterday	**kemarin**
today	**hari ini**
tomorrow	**bésok**
the day after tomorrow	**lusa**

last week	**minggu yang lalu, minggu kemarin**
last Thursday	**hari Kamis yang lalu**
last month	**bulan yang lalu**
last year	**tahun lalu**
next week	**minggu depan**
next month	**bulan depan**
next year	**tahun depan**

Tadi is a very useful word to refer to a time that has just passed.

last night	**tadi malam**
(earlier) this morning	**tadi pagi**
(earlier) this afternoon	**tadi siang, tadi soré**
just now	**tadi**

For lengths of time, simply switch the word order to number and hours (**jam**).

6 hours	**enam jam**
6 o'clock	**jam enam**

▶ How long have you been in Indonesia?
  Sudah berapa lama di Indonésia?

three days	**sudah tiga hari**
one week	**sudah seminggu**
not long	**belum lama**

Sudah (*already*) is also a tense marker for past events or actions.

  Sedang (*-ing, in the act of*) marks present, current actions.

  Belum (*not yet*) is often used instead of **tidak** (*no*). For instance, a 60-year-old might optimistically say that he is not married: **Saya belum kawin**. **Belum** is a useful, diplomatic and evasive way to avoid possibly hard facts.

Special Dates
Dates are formed from the word **tanggal** (*date*), before a number then month (as can be done in English).

14 October, October the 14th, October 14	**tanggal empat belas Oktober**
1 January (New Year's Day)	**tanggal satu Januari**
17 August (Independence Day)	**tanggal tujuh belas Agustus (Hari Kemerdékaan)**
1 September	**tanggal satu Séptémber**
10 November (Heroes Day)	**tanggal sepuluh Novémber (Hari Pahlawan)**

MONTHS

January	**bulan Januari**
February	**bulan Fébruari**
March	**bulan Maret**
April	**bulan April**
May	**bulan Méi**
June	**bulan Juni**
July	**bulan Juli**
August	**bulan Agustus**
September	**bulan Séptémber**
October	**bulan Oktober**
November	**bulan Novémber**
December	**bulan Désémber**

YEARS

year	**tahun**
decade	**dasawarsa, sepuluh tahun**
century	**abad**
1952 (nineteen fifty-two)	**tahun sembilan belas lima puluh dua**
1952 (one thousand nine hundred and fifty-two)	**tahun seribu sembilan ratus lima puluh dua**
2008	**tahun dua ribu delapan**
2011	**tahun dua ribu sebelas**

▶ What is your date of birth?
   Tanggal lahirnya kapan?

▶ When is your birthday?
   Kapan ulang tahunnya?

▶ 1 September 1985.
   Tanggal satu Séptémber tahun sembilan belas delapan lima

Years can be said either as the exact year (one thousand nine hundred and seventy-four) or divided into two-digit numbers (nineteen seventy-four). Years from 2000 onwards are known as **dua ribu ...** (two thousand and ...). Use the word **tahun** (*year*) before the number, for clarity.

Other "moving" holidays include Chinese New Year (**Imlék**) in late January / early February, Good Friday (**Jumat Agung**) and *Waisak* (Buddha's birthday) in April or May. The biggest of these is Idul Fitri or Lebaran, which (as of 2015) fell in July, when most businesses close for a week and huge numbers of people choke all forms of transportation as they return to their village for celebrations. It is advised to seriously reconsider any long-distance movement within Indonesia at this time. Idul Fitri is preceded by the fasting month of Ramadan, when many restaurants close during the day and there are many religious activities. Idul Adha, the Feast of the Sacrifice, falls approximately two months after Idul Fitri.

WEATHER

▶ What season is it?
Sekarang musim apa?

the wet season	**musim hujan**
the dry season	**musim kemarau**
between seasons	**musim pancaroba**

▶ How many seasons are there in your country?
Di negara anda ada berapa musim?

two seasons	**dua musim**
four seasons	**empat musim**
spring	**musim semi, musim bunga**
summer	**musim panas**
autumn	**musim gugur**
winter	**musim dingin**
snow season	**musim salju**

▶ What will the weather be like today?
Bagaimana cuaca hari ini?

clear	**cerah**
cloudy	**mendung, berawan**
cool	**sejuk**
cold	**dingin**
dry	**kering**
fog	**kabut**
hail	**hujan és**
hot	**panas**
light rain, drizzle	**gerimis**
lightning	**petir, halilintar**
rainy	**hujan**
smog, pollution	**polusi, asap**
storm	**badai**
thunder	**geludug, guntur**
typhoon	**badai topan**
warm	**hangat**
weather forecast	**prakiraan cuaca**
wind	**angin**

▶ Will I need a <u>jacket</u>?
Apa perlu saya bawa <u>jakét</u>?

| umbrella | **payung** |
| warm clothes | **baju hangat** |

There are only really two seasons in Indonesia, the wet and the dry. The rains used to last from September to April, before the dry season kicked in, but with climate change this rough guide to the seasons is much less certain.

Weather in Indonesia rarely changes from being hot (around 25°C to 32°C). Rain is perhaps the only occasionally unpredictable factor. Mountain areas can be several degrees cooler, requiring jackets at night.

COMMUNICATIONS

Phone, Email & Internet

▶ I want to buy a mobile phone.
Saya mau beli ponsél / hapé.

▶ I want to buy a card for my mobile phone.
Saya mau beli kartu SIM untuk ponsél.

▶ What is the cheapest package?
Kartu mana yang paling murah?

▶ Which package is the best deal?
Kartu mana yang pakétnya paling bagus?

▶ Which package has the best signal locally?
Kartu mana yang sinyalnya paling kuat di sini?

▶ Which package has the best signal in Java?
Kartu mana yang sinyalnya paling kuat di Jawa?

in Sumatra	**di Sumatera**
in eastern Indonesia	**di Indonésia bagian timur**
in Bali	**di pulau Bali**
in Kalimantan	**di Kalimantan**

▶ What card is suitable for this phone?
Kartu mana yang cocok bagi ponsél ini?

▶ Can I buy top-up credit?
Apa saya bisa beli pulsa?

Rp.50.000 credit	**pulsa lima puluh ribu (rupiah)**
Rp.100.000 credit	**pulsa seratus ribu (rupiah)**

▶ How can I send a text?
Bagaimana bisa mengirim SMS? [read *es-em-es*]

▶ How can I send an email?
Bagaimana bisa mengirim imél?

▶ How can I connect to the Internet?
Bagaimana bisa menyambung ke internét?

Indonesians are great communicators who have enthusiastically welcomed the advent of mobile phones and social media, The level of mobile saturation across the country is so high that you will see not just professionals and young go-getters, but old ladies, young children and village women busy with their mobile devices. Texting and social media is very popular as it is cheap.

You can buy a phone (SIM) card easily without having to buy a phone as well. Look for stalls with names such as Telkomsel, Esia, Mentari, etc. Unfortunately, this means public landline phones are hard to come by. There is still the odd **wartél** (telephone office) but you would be better advised to bring your own device and buy a local card for it.

▶ Is there a public phone around here?
Apa ada télepon umum dekat sini?

▶ Where can I make a long-distance call?
Di mana saya bisa télepon SLJJ?

local call	**télepon lokal**
long-distance call	**télepon SLJJ** [letters read as in English] **(sambungan langsung jarak jauh)**
international call	**télepon SLI** [*es el ee*] **(sambungan langsung internasional)**

▶ Where can I send a fax?
Di mana saya bisa kirim faks?

As mentioned, public phones are few and far between. Local calls used to be made with gold-colored coins (Rp.100, Rp.200 and Rp.500) but these have also been replaced by feather-light silver coins unsuitable for public phones. Phone cards were once quite common but have faded away with the saturation of mobile coverage and users. Your best bet (if you don't have your own cell phone) is to look for a public phone office (**wartél**)—whose days are also rapidly numbered.

Some large **wartél** used to act as **warpostél** that also offered postal services. Again, technology has resulted in their decline, although post offices are still fairly well spread across the country, particularly in rural areas, and can also be used to send money.

▶ I would like to send ... .
  Saya mau kirim ... .

a fax	**faks, faksimili**
letter	**surat**
money	**uang**
a package	**pakét**
postcard	**kartu pos**
via	**pakai**
air mail	**pos udara**
express mail	**éksprés**
registered post	**pos tercatat**

If you are a fan of sending postcards, be aware that this is not a particularly strong tradition in Indonesia (unlike Japan, or Europe). If you see postcards for sale, buy them immediately, even if they show places you haven't been to yet! They are nearly always available at Periplus bookshops.

Repairs
▶ My <u>phone</u> isn't working.
  <u>**Télepon**</u> **saya rusak.**

tablet	**tablét**
laptop	**komputer jinjing, laptop**
computer	**komputer**

▶ Do you know where I can service a Nokia phone?
Di mana bisa sérvis télepon Nokia?

▶ Could I please charge my phone?
Boléh isi ponsél? Boléh ngecas HP [*ha pe*]**?**

▶ I would like to buy a charger for my phone.
Saya mau beli *charger* ponsél.

With limited language skills, it is better to stick to
"official" repair outlets rather than take your chances
elsewhere. Do not expect that any guarantees and
warranties will be automatically accepted. Make sure
you can communicate properly before anything is
done to your phone.

It is quite common to use any available socket to
charge a phone, even in public places like hospitals
or restaurants. Where possible, you should of course
ask permission first (**Boléh diisi / dicas?**).

Wi-fi
▶ Do you have Wi-fi here?
Apa ada *wi-fi* di sini?

▶ What is the Wi-fi password?
Kata sandi untuk *wi-fi* apa ya?

▶ I would like to use the Internet.
Saya mau pakai internét.

▶ How much for one hour?
Berapa biayanya untuk satu jam?

▶ I would like to print something.
Saya mau ngeprint / mencétak sesuatu.

Unlike in some Western countries, Wi-fi is ubiquitous in hotels and many cafes and eateries, although you may have to ask for the password. If there is a fee, it is usually small.

Internet services can be found at business centers in larger hotels, or Internet cafes (**warnét**).

Social media

social media	**média sosial, sosméd**
Twitter	**Twitter**
to tweet	**ngetwit**
tweet	**twit**

▶ Are you on Twitter?
Apa sudah aktif di *Twitter*?

▶ Are you on Facebook?
Apa ada di Facebook / fésbuk?

▶ Can I friend you on Facebook?
Boleh jadi teman di Facebook / fésbuk?

▶ What's your phone number?
Berapa nomor téleponnya?

▶ This is my mobile number.
Ini nomor ponsél saya.

▶ This is my home number.
Ini nomor télepon rumah saya.

▶ I'll ring you when I get there.
Nanti kalau sudah sampai, saya télepon.

▶ I'll text you when I get there.
Nanti kalau sudah sampai, saya kirim SMS
[letters read as in English]

▶ I'll send you a missed call.
Nanti saya miskol.

▶ Sorry, my battery died.
Maaf, baterainya habis.

▶ Sorry, my phone wasn't working.
Maaf, téleponnya rusak.

▶ Sorry, my phone was turned off.
Maaf, téleponnya mati.

▶ Sorry, my phone was on silent mode.
Maaf, téleponnya sedang *silent*.

▶ Sorry, there was no signal.
Maaf, tidak ada sinyal.

If you do not want to keep in touch with someone, you can always offer the following excuses.

▶ Sorry, I'm not on Facebook / Twitter.
Maaf, saya tidak ada di fésbuk / *Twitter*.

▶ I don't know my cellphone number.
Saya tidak hafal nomor hapé saya.

▶ What's your number? I'll send you it later.
Berapa nomornya? Nanti saya kirim.

▶ My phone's dead right now.
Saat ini télepon saya sedang mati.

▶ I'm going home tomorrow.
  Saya sudah mau pulang bésok.

Indonesians have one of the world's highest social
media usage and number of Facebook accounts per
capita. People are sure to invite you to stay in touch.

MEDICAL

▶ I feel sick / tired / aching all over / nauseous.
  **Saya ... tidak énak badan / capék / pegal-pegal /
  mual.**

▶ Do you have anything for ... ?
  Apa ada obat untuk ... ?

asthma	**asma, sesak napas**
athlete's foot	**jamur**
backache	**sakit pinggang**
blisters	**luka lécét**
a cold	**pilek, selesma**
constipation	**sembelit**
diarrhea	**diaré, méncrét**
earache	**sakit telinga**
fever	**demam**
flu	**flu**
hayfever	**alérgi**

headache	**sakit kepala**
jellyfish stings	**ruam ubur-ubur**
menstrual pain	**sakit méns**
migraine	**sakit kepala migrén**
mouth ulcers	**sariawan**
mosquito bites	**gigitan nyamuk**
nausea	**mual**
a runny nose	**hidung mélér**
sinusitis	**sakit sinus**
sore throat	**sakit tenggorokan**
toothache	**sakit gigi**

▶ I wear / use ... .
Saya pakai ... .

contact lenses	**lénsa kontak**
false teeth	**gigi palsu**
glasses	**kacamata**
a hearing aid	**alat bantu dengar**
a pacemaker	**alat pacu jantung**
an IUD	**spiral**
a wheelchair	**kursi roda**

▶ I'm looking for ....
Saya mencari ....

anti-mosquito cream	**obat nyamuk, krim anti nyamuk**

a bandage	**perban**
cold and flu medicine	**obat pilek, obat flu**
contact lens solution	**cairan lénsa kontak**
cotton balls	**kapas**
cotton buds	**korék kuping**
dental floss	**pita gigi, benang gigi**
deodorant	**déodoran**
eye drops	**tétés mata**
a face mask	**masker**
laxatives	**obat peluntur**
methylated spirits	**alkohol, spiritus**
nursing pads	**bantalan menyusui**
paracetamol	**parasétamol**
sanitary pads	**pembalut (wanita)**
sleeping pills	**obat tidur**
sticking plasters	**pléster, hansaplast**
talcum powder	**bedak**
throat lozenges	**obat isap buat tenggorokan**
tranquillizers	**obat penenang**

▶ I would like to see the <u>doctor</u>.
Saya mau berobat ke <u>dokter</u>.

acupuncturist	**ahli tusuk jarum**
dentist	**dokter gigi**
nurse	**perawat**
pediatrician	**dokter anak**
specialist	**intérnis, dokter ahli**

▶ I've been sick for three days.
Saya sudah sakit selama tiga hari.

▶ It hurts here.
Sakit di sini.

▶ I just want to sleep.
Saya hanya ingin tidur.

▶ I don't feel like eating.
Saya malas makan.

▶ You need to rest.
Anda perlu istirahat.

▶ You need a night in hospital.
Anda perlu diopname / dirawat.

▶ You need a blood test.
Anda perlu tés darah.

▶ It could be ....
Mungkin ....

dengue fever	**demam berdarah**
malaria	**malaria**
typhoid fever	**tifus, tipus**
a virus	**virus**

alternative/Chinese medicine	**obat altérnatif, obat Cina**
antibiotics	**antibiotik**
medicine	**obat**
vitamins	**vitamin**
take after meals	**sesudah makan**
take before meals	**sebelum makan**
finish the medicine	**habiskan**

▶ I don't want antibiotics.
Saya tidak mau antibiotik.

▶ I'm allergic to ...
Saya ada alérgi terhadap ...

▶ I'm breastfeeding.
Saya menyusui.

▶ I'm diabetic.
Saya diabét.

▶ I'm on the pill.
Saya minum pil kontrasépsi.

▶ I'm pregnant.
Saya hamil.

If you end up at the doctor's, you may have to wait in a queue. Local clinics are usually very cheap; more expensive establishments in big cities and hospitals cost more but are also far more likely to have English-speaking doctors.

Going to the doctor can be very stressful if you don't know the language. Sometimes, if you think you know what's wrong, a pharmacy (**apotik, apoték**) may be your first port of call. Pharmacies in shopping malls are more likely to have English-speaking staff than small doctors' surgeries practicing in the evening.

EMERGENCIES

▶ Help!
  Tolong!

▶ What are you doing?
  Lagi apa? / Lagi ngapain?

▶ Don't do that.
  Jangan.

▶ Stop it now.
  Hentikan. Stop.

▶ I don't like it.
  Saya tidak suka.

▶ My wallet!
  Dompét saya!

▶ My phone!
  Hapé saya!

▶ My camera!
  Kaméra saya!

▶ I've been robbed!
  Saya dirampok! (with force) /
  Saya kecopétan! (pickpocketed)

▶ It's been stolen!
  Saya kecurian!

▶ Fire!
  Kebakaran!

▶ Earthquake!
  Gempa bumi!

▶ Flood!
  Banjir!

MY BAG!!!
TAS SAYA!!!

HELP!!!
TOLONG!!!

I'VE BEEN MUGGED!!!
SAYA DIRAMPOK!!!

Are you okay, Miss?
Tidak apa-apa, Nona?

Please help me!
Tolong saya!

Calm down. Let's report this to the police.
Tenang, ayo kita lapor polisi dulu.

▶ There's water everywhere.
Ada air di mana-mana.

▶ I've lost my luggage.
Bagasi saya hilang.

▶ I've lost my ticket.
Karcis / Tikét saya hilang.

▶ I don't have any money.
Saya tidak ada uang.

▶ I need a doctor.
Saya mau cari dokter.

▶ Where is the police station?
Di mana kantor polisi?

▶ Where is the hospital?
Di mana rumah sakit?

▶ I want to report a crime.
Saya mau melapor.

▶ I've been pickpocketed.
Saya dicopét.

▶ I've been groped.
Saya dipégang-pégang.

▶ I've been assaulted.
Saya dipukuli.

▶ I've been raped.
Saya diperkosa.

▶ I want an interpreter.
Saya minta penterjemah.

▶ I want to make a phone call.
Saya mau bertélepon.

▶ I've done nothing wrong.
Saya tidak bersalah.

Despite occasional negative press overseas, Indonesia is generally a very safe place for tourists, and most people are friendly and helpful. As with anywhere, you should always guard your personal belongings safely, and be cautious in busy public places such as markets, bus terminals and railway stations. Hopefully none of the above will happen to you. Apart from losing personal items, the most likely situation you may encounter is that of flooding, which happens frequently during the rainy season (and sometimes at other times). In an emergency, often the most useful port of call is your hotel reception desk, as your welfare is their concern and they will probably have prior experience of problems.

PART THREE

Exploring Indonesia

PUBLIC HOLIDAYS AND FESTIVALS

There are fourteen official national holidays in Indonesia (as of 2016), some of which are important religious or cultural celebrations for the public, others which most people appreciate as an opportunity for a day off work or school. As with any holidays, some are more important than others, depending on who you are. Interestingly (and quite usefully), most shopping malls open on public holidays, with the exception of the first day of Lebaran (Idul Fitri).

New Year's Eve (*Malam Tahun Baru*, 31 December)
In Indonesia, New Year's Eve has become an increasingly popular celebration in the 21st century, especially with young people. Planned events in large hotels which include entertainment, games, fireworks and other activities leading up to counting in the new year at midnight are inspiring more spontaneous celebrations in public places. New Year's Eve coverage on national television is also becoming more and more extensive. The evening of 31 December, which was once only noted by westernized Indonesians, often of Dutch

descent or Christian religion, is now moving into the
mainstream.

**Chinese New Year (*Imlék, Cap Go Méh*, late January–
mid-February)**
Chinese New Year has a poignant meaning in modern
Indonesia, as any open celebrations of it were banned
during the New Order years between 1967 and 1998.
This was one form of discrimination against Indonesia's
ethnic Chinese minority, who make up just 3 percent of
the population but wield considerable economic influence. Historically Indonesian Chinese have been Hok-
kien-speaking settlers along the east coast of Sumatra
and north coast of Java and their descendants, although
Chinese are to be found throughout the archipelago.
In the 20th century a greater variety of Chinese im-
migrants arrived, lending local colour and diversity to
Chinese New Year celebrations around the country.
   A highlight of Chinese New Year celebrations are
the dancing lions, known as **barongsai**. These involve
young men (occasionally women) dancing and leap-
ing on raised pillars while wearing the dragon costume
on their heads—this means they are often jumping
blind. **Barongsai** groups practice throughout the year
for **Imlék**, and a particularly Indonesian touch is that
they are not restricted to ethnic Chinese. Some of the
best **barongsai** artists are local Muslims. **Barongsai**
are often accompanied by **liong**, where the long dragon

is held aloft with sticks and wound around in intricate patterns by its puppeteers. And of course, it would not be Chinese New Year without fireworks.

Traditionally, Chinese families will visit the temple before gathering in families for a hearty meal and exchange of *angpao* or lucky money. This may be at home or in a restaurant. The little red envelopes of money can be given to any child or young adult before they marry, and are often even given to non-Chinese! Fifteen days into Chinese New Year, the celebration **Cap Go Méh** is held, marking the next phase of the moon. A special dish, **lontong cap go méh**, is made from vegetables in a spicy soup accompanied by rice cakes. There may also be street parades but the whole affair is much more low-key than Chinese New Year.

Nyepi (**Balinese Day of Silence**, March)
Indonesia's remaining Hindus, dating from Majapahit times, are concentrated in Bali and smaller pockets across Central and East Java. The differences between Hinduism in Indonesia and in India are clear, with various rites and rituals having been retained from the past as well as adapted and modified by indigenous practices. One example is **Nyepi**, where Hindus spend 24 hours without only speaking, but also avoiding electricity, cooking or any work other than praying or quiet reflection. This has obvious implications for the tourist island of Bali, where there are no incoming or outgo-

ing flights on the Day of Silence, and hotels basically shut down to a minimum service staffed by non-Hindus. Hindus also visit the temple and give offerings at this time.

Good Friday (*Jumat Agung*)

This date is as important in the Christian (and Catholic—there is a distinction made in Indonesia) calendar as in the West. Church-going Indonesians will attend a service or mass, while for some, the fast of Lent will be over. Easter Sunday is enthusiastically celebrated by Christians and Catholics, and is particularly evident in eastern Indonesia. Interestingly, Easter Monday is no longer celebrated as a public holiday, although in the past it had been permitted as a day off for Catholics and Christians.

May Day (*Hari Buruh*, 1 May)

This is a relatively new public holiday and perhaps reflects a traditionally strong sense of sympathy for the **orang kecil**, or ordinary person. Currently it seems to be marked by workers' marches, and the odd demonstration which mostly passes without incident.

Isra Miraj (currently in May)

This day is related to Allah's revelation to the Prophet Muhammad regarding the performing of the five daily prayers.

Ascension Day (*Kenaikan Isa Almasih*, currently in May)
This date marks Jesus' ascension to Heaven forty days after his crucifixion, and always falls on a Thursday.

Waisak (May/June)
Perhaps due to Indonesia's relatively small number of Buddhists, **Waisak** (Visakh) is not as widely celebrated as in other southeast Asian countries. It falls on a full moon, usually during May, and commemorates the birth of Siddharta Gautama, his reaching enlightenment, and the death of the Buddha. Celebrations center on Borobudur temple in Central Java, involving meditation, parades and alms-giving.

Ramadan (currently June-July)
The Muslim holy month is by no means a holiday, but is worthy of inclusion for the impact it has on daily life in most parts of Indonesia. The excitement on the first day of fasting is palpable, even if you are not fasting! For thirty days, Muslims are required to abstain from food, drink and impure thoughts (including anger and sex!) during daylight hours from dawn to dusk. During the first two weeks of fasting, life pretty much continues as usual, with most schools and workplaces operating as normal. You will notice that many restaurants hang curtains around their windows in deference to the large number of people fasting. The last two weeks of fasting

see a gradual draining of the big cities as people return to their villages or ancestral homes to prepare for **Idul Fitri**. This huge temporary migration is known colloquially as **mudik** ("going upstream") and is one of the world's largest annual mass movements of humanity. The final week of Ramadan sees schools and businesses closing for the upcoming holiday.

For those fasting, the holy month is an opportunity to improve oneself, with added emphasis on performing the five daily prayers, reading the Koran, performing good deeds and attending evening prayers at the mosque. Evening prayers are particularly well-attended by women, and also children, who are not normally seen at Friday prayers. While not quite a party atmosphere, there is a distinct feeling of solidarity and occasion as Muslims wake up in the middle of the night to cook and eat before dawn, and then try to maintain their everyday activities before finally gathering to break the fast (**buka puasa**), often with friends, family or workmates at home or in a restaurant. If you are invited to a **buka puasa**, it is a wonderful opportunity to sample delicious local food, some specific to Ramadan, such as **biji salak** or **kolak**.

Idul Fitri (**Eid, Eid ul-Fitr**, also known as *Hari Raya* or **Lebaran**, currently July)
The first day after Ramadan (1 Syawwal) is the one day that stops the nation, literally. All businesses (save ho-

tels and hospitals) are closed and not even the cinemas open. People rush to return to their homes so that they can perform the **Idul Fitri** mass prayer with their family. The early morning sight of thousands of people praying in the street—only the lucky, early few get a space in the mosque—is truly memorable. A particularly Indonesian tradition is to ask forgiveness of one another on this day, for past wrongs, intended or accidental (**"mohon maaf lahir dan batin"**). Another tradition is to visit the graves of family members and lay flowers. And of course there is the feasting: every region has its own specialty, but beef rendang, **sambal goréng ati** (spicy liver) and **opor ayam** (chicken in coconut soup) are perhaps the most famous delicacies. People who lost weight during fasting have been known to put it straight back on in only two days of **Idul Fitri**!

Daily activities slowly return to normal after a few days, and everyone is back to the daily grind at work or school by a fortnight. It is strongly recommended to avoid travel in the week before and after **Idul Fitri** … unless you are accompanying someone home to the village, or feeling adventurous. This is the best time of the year to visit Jakarta, which is pleasantly empty and devoid of traffic jams for around two weeks after having been deserted by two to three million of its population.

Independence Day (17 August)

As Japan limped towards ultimate defeat, Indonesian freedom fighters declared independence on 17 August 1945, although full and universal recognition only came later. This date is enthusiastically celebrated across the nation, especially outside large cities. Various competitions are held, such as decorating bicycles, climbing greasy poles to gather prizes, eating krupuk crackers hung by a string and so on. If there is nothing exciting happening locally, you can always watch the telecast from Merdéka Palace as the President presides over the raising of the red and white flag to parades and performances by groups from across the country.

Idul Adha (**Feast of the Sacrifice,** currently September)

This is the second big Islamic festival after **Idul Fitri**, held on the day when pilgrims to Mecca reach Arafah. Again, the day starts with mass prayers, but after this the main event is the slaughtering of goats and cows, symbolizing Ibrahim's (Abraham in English) willingness to sacrifice his son Ismail (Ishmael). Goat dishes such as **tongséng** and **gulai kambing** are key delicacies served at **Idul Adha**. The meat is then divided by the family or distributed to the poor. Many Indonesians return home to the village but the exodus is far smaller than during Idul Fitri.

Islamic New Year (*Tahun Baru Hijriah*, currently towards the end of the year)
This marks the new year, according to the Islamic calendar, which dates from the time of the Prophet Muhammad rather than 0 AD. 2016 will be the Islamic year 1437. Celebrations are fairly low-key.

Maulid Nabi (**Prophet's Birthday**, approaching year's end)
The first day of the Islamic month Muharram is celebrated widely in central Java, where it is known as Muludan. The festival Sekaten was started by one of Java's nine holy men to help encourage the locals to follow the new religion of Islam by incorporating a number of Javanese elements.

Christmas (*Natal*, 25 December)
Christmas is widely celebrated across Indonesia, particularly in the bigger cities and in Christian or Catholic majority areas such as North Sumatra, North Sulawesi, Papua and much of eastern Indonesia. Shopping malls are decked out in glitter and tinsel long beforehand, as in much of the modern world. For Indonesian believers, Christmas is a religious rather than cultural celebration, and present-giving is not particularly widespread. For others, Christmas is an opportunity to enjoy Dutch-inspired cooking and delicious cakes.

Pangandaran kite festival (dry season, April–August)
The age-old children's tradition of flying kites during
the dry season is celebrated at this now annual event
held for the past twenty years or so. Various competitions are held involving participants from Asia and beyond. The sheer variety of sizes, colors and designs of
kites soaring high above are worth the trip down to this
small port on the south coast of West Java.

Nyalé (**Sea Worms Festival**, February, Lombok)
This festival is known in the Sasak community of Lombok and also on nearby Sumba, when villagers come
down to the shore to catch sea worms (**nyalé**) which
only appear at this time of year. The story goes that long
ago, Mandalika, a local princess, flung herself into the
sea; yet when her people tried to fish her out, all they
collected were sea worms. A number of cultural activities are held, including boat races and parades.

POPULAR DESTINATIONS

There is much to do and see in Indonesia, where the
different regions offer different types of fun and exciting adventures to different groups of travelers. The following destinations are grouped by thematic interests,
rather than by geographical regions.

BEACHES

Bali

Bali is Indonesia's prima donna tourist destination, with millions of foreign visitors every year, not to mention its huge popularity with Indonesians, especially the burgeoning middle class. Bali's attraction lies in its exotic Hindu culture, unique in the world, and to some degree its "party" atmosphere. While some may tire of the increasing commercialization of life, particularly down south, the island has something to offer any budget, from glamorous high-end villas in Nusa Dua to yoga, alternative lifestyles and a writer's festival in Ubud or snorkeling and diving off the black beaches on Bali's north coast.

Bali's most celebrated tourist destinations are the temples of Tanah Lot (surrounded by sea when the tide is in), Bedugul in the cool climate of Lake Bratan, and Besakih, halfway up sacred Mount Agung. Water sports (including surfing) are popular everywhere, including on the beautiful Nusa Penida just a short ferry ride away from Sanur. You can feed and marvel at naughty monkeys at the Monkey Forest at Sangeh, or enjoy the breathtaking views from the clifftops at Uluwati on Bali's southern tip. A glimpse of life in Bali as it used to be can be seen in the regional towns of Singaraja, Karangasem and Klungkung.

Bali is serviced by flights from around Indonesia and southeast Asia, and can be reached from Surabaya by train (connecting with a bus), and ferry from East Java and Lombok.

Lombok

A much larger island than its western neighbor Bali, Lombok is vastly different both in terms of geography as well as its Sasak culture. On the Australasian side of the Wallace Line running between the two islands, its landscape has more of a savannah, dry feel similar to islands further east instead of the lush, tropical climes of western Indonesia. Lombok is strongly Muslim, with extensive pockets of immigrant Balinese communities. Many tourists enjoy relatively secluded beaches at Senggigi and Kuta, while Mount Rinjani offers hiking possibilities. Lombok is famous for its weavings and also pottery.

Lombok is easily reached from Bali by ferry or plane, and has a number of other air links to Jakarta and other cities. A ferry also connects to Sumbawa, the next island east.

Belitung

The previously forgotten island of Belitung (or Billiton, as Raffles knew it), once famous for its tin mines, entered the national consciousness after the publication of Andrea Hirata's hit novel *The Rainbow Troops* (**Laskar Pelangi**) about growing up poor on the island. This revived interest in Belitung's fascinating mix of Malay and Chinese culture as well as its pristine, spectacular beaches (and, less encouragingly, environmental threats.)

Belitung is part of Sumatra but actually lies slightly east of Jakarta in the Java Sea. It is easily accessible by air or by ferry from neighboring Bangka. Together they form the province of Bangka-Belitung (Babel).

Raja Ampat

Raja Ampat (literally, "four kings") is high on the list of serious divers looking for unspoilt waters and clear views of incredibly diverse marine life. Most visitors come to dive, and stay either in resorts, on boats or in local homestays. Other activities include bushwalking, exploring the islands by boat, learning about the local culture and seeing beautiful waterfalls as well as perhaps a bird of paradise.

Raja Ampat is located near Sorong on the Bird's Head peninsula in West Papua. There are flights from Jakarta, Makassar and Manado as well as Bali (Denpasar). The political situation in Papua (formerly Irian Jaya) means that there is more red tape than usual for foreign visitors, such as gaining a permit from the police before you go diving.

Manado

Manado (Menado) is the capital of North Sulawesi, a far-flung province that feels vastly different to Muslim-majority Java. Here, life has been heavily influenced by Dutch, Western and Christian culture, as seen from the proliferation of churches, a drinking culture and beautiful local embroidery. Manadonese food is famously spicy and its distinctive local dishes center on seafood, but also include bat and sometimes even dog. Visitors to Manado can travel to the excellent Bunaken marine park to dive or snorkel, as well as the Minahasa highlands around Tomohon (famous for its flowers) and Lake Tondano. Manado can be reached by air from Jakarta, Makassar and Singapore.

Thousand Islands (Pulau Seribu)
For an escape from Jakarta's smog and grit, the Thousand Islands (actually only 128) are an often-forgotten alternative. Just 45 minutes by boat from the Ancol entertainment complex in North Jakarta, there are a variety of islands for different pursuits, mainly focusing on water sports. Diving is popular on Kotok, while the turtle breeding farm and community programs on Pramuka are also worth a visit. The islands of Bidadari, Ayer, Sepa and Putri are among the most popular. Accommodation ranges from homestays to classier hotels and "resorts."

MOUNTAINS

Bandung
Known in Dutch times as the "Paris of Java," Bandung still retains an elegance and charm despite chronic traffic and increasing pollution. Located on the Priangan plain at 709 m above sea level, the temperature is 2–3 degrees cooler than Jakarta and cool at night.

Bandung is home to the Sundanese people, whose language is related to but distinct from the majority Javanese. Sundanese cuisine is famous for its vegetables and freshness, and there are many excellent eateries around.

In town, there is the Geology Museum (covering dinosaurs to earthquakes), **angklung** performances and fashionable factory outlets to keep visitors busy. Bandung boasts several excellent day trips, such as to the hot springs at Ciater, Ciwidey or Garut, walking trails near the Maribaya waterfall, or the distinctive Tangkuban Parahu volcano. The cool mountain town of Lembang on the way home from the crater is also worth a stop.

Although the majority arrive by car, the scenic train journey to Bandung from Jakarta takes just under three hours and winds through some of the most beautiful valleys, paddy fields and ravines you will see. There are also train and air links from Surabaya and Jogjakarta.

Puncak

Over the years, development and urbanization have not dimmed public enthusiasm for Puncak as a weekend escape from Jakarta. While the main road is tarnished by endless advertising and urban sprawl, once up on the mountain the view of the velvety tea plantations below is still spectacular, if there is no fog. The brisk climate and friendly local Sundanese people make Puncak a favorite place for holiday houses and villas. Visitors can explore tea plantations and go on a "tea walk," while stopping for roasted corn on the cob and spicy ginger drinks is a timeless tradition. On the Cianjur side of Puncak Pass, the Cibodas Botanic Gardens (less well-known than their famous Bogor cousin) is well worth a visit, and is also the starting point for a day walk up and back to the Cibeureum waterfall on Mount Gede.

Most people visit Puncak by car. Otherwise you can take the train from Jakarta to Bogor, then a blue **angkot** with the destination "Cisarua."

Malang

Like Bandung, Malang is a cool, former colonial hill town. And (like Bandung) despite having developed into a much larger urban sprawl, the town center still retains much charm for the visitor. Around the famous **tugu** (monument) near the railway station lie various hotels and places to eat, as well as attractive streets winding around the River Brantas, waiting to be explored. Toko Oen on Jl. Basuki Rahmat is also a must for its colonial decor and delicious food. Outside the city, the resort town of Batu has developed in recent years, boasting a zoo, various hotels, orchards and a safari park. A little further afield lie the rocky southern beaches, Mount Arjuna and Mount Kelud, and the town of Blitar, resting place of President Sukarno.

Malang is within two hours drive of Surabaya (less if direct from Juanda airport), or an hour's flight from Jakarta direct into Malang. The train journey from central Java is more circuitous but emphasizes Malang's location as a regional center. Taxis are widely available.

Bukittinggi

While Padang proves too hot for many foreign tourists, Bukittinggi lies in the much cooler Minangkabau highlands and is located central to many interesting sights. The town itself boasts a strange, atmospheric canyon (Ngarai Sianok) as well as a night market, winding cobbled streets and access to the Pagaruyung palace in Batusangkar, the Harau valley, two lakes (Maninjau and Singkarak), and Sawahlunto, where a steam train still runs to Padang and back. The local satay is a specialty, and you can find various examples of Minangkabau culture such as traditional dance, **talémpong** music and woven **songkét**.

Bukittinggi is a two-hour drive or bus ride from Padang.

ADVENTURE

Kalimantan

The huge island of Kalimantan (or Borneo, as the English knew it) is one of the largest in the world, and impossible to cover adequately in a paragraph. Visitors to Kalimantan often head for orangutan protection centers in Central and South Kalimantan, and trips up the river by boat. Treks through or visits to the jungle should include time spent at a traditional longhouse where indigenous people (once known as Dayak) live. The floating market at Banjarmasin in South Kalimantan is also a

popular tourist attraction. Souvenirs include distinctive tie-dye batik (**sasirangan**) and precious gems—the name Kalimantan means "river of diamonds."

There are several flights a day from Jakarta to Pontianak, Banjarmasin and Balikpapan, the three largest cities.

Aceh

Aceh's history changed irreversibly on 26 December, 2004 when a massive tsunami hit the province, killing over 10,000 people. Ironically, the devastation that followed achieved a number of positive outcomes, one of which was massive reconstruction, and another political peace. The huge influx of overseas aid workers resulted in a new, foreigner-friendly Aceh constructed to 21st century standards, greatly encouraging the growth of tourism. The effects of the tsunami can still be seen throughout much of the capital Banda Aceh and coastal towns. Huge ships stranded among public buildings have become tourist attractions; and the impressive Tsunami Museum (one of Indonesia's best museums) gives an excellent idea of what happened in a multi-sensory approach. Delicious local food and unbeatable coffee also make Aceh a tempting destination.

Just 45 minutes from Banda Aceh by ferry is the island of Weh, commonly known as Sabang (its capital), where breathtaking views of the ocean and picturesque hamlets greet the visitor. Sabang is also a haven for diving, and famous for being Indonesia's western extremity (you can visit Kilometer 0 on the island's westerly tip). While local and Indonesian women are expected to cover their heads, there is less compulsion on foreign women to do so.

There are daily flights to Aceh from Medan and Jakarta; by bus or car from Medan takes 10–12 hours.

Lake Toba
This enormous lake, once the crater of an even more gigantic volcano, is the pride of North Sumatra and its Batak people. The scenery is wild and rugged, much

like the Batak character. Around the perimeter of the
lake and on the island of Samosir, you will see many
churches and unusual, highly decorative graves. Visitors
can stay in Parapat, a well-equipped town on the eastern
shore, or take a ferry over to Samosir, where a number
of hotels crowd along the Tuktuk peninsula. The Sipiso-
piso waterfall along the lake's northern perimeter is
also worth a visit. Cultural visits to Batak villages also
reveal a unique way of life with distinctive architecture.
The most famous local handicraft is the woven **ulos**,
which has great significance in Batak culture.

   Lake Toba is around four hours' travel time by car or
bus from Medan.

Komodo

An increasingly popular destination over the past few
years, the island of Komodo and its neighbors, Rinca
and Padar, provide an exciting and unforgettable experience. The chief at-
traction, of course, is
the ancient Komodo
dragons which still
roam the islands. The
dry, rugged land-
scape clearly shares
more in common
with that of Australia
than of the tropical

Southeast Asian geography of Java, Kalimantan and Sumatra.

A trip to Komodo should include the boat journey, whether from Labuan Bajo on Flores or Sapa on Sumbawa, with accommodation usually provided on board. Flights are available from Bali or other cities in eastern Indonesia.

Ambon

One of Indonesia's lesser-known gems, Maluku (Moluccas) province is home to the original Spice Islands of Ternate and Tidore, over which Western empires once fought. These tiny islands are centered on spectacular Mount Gamalama and grow nutmeg, mace and cloves. A short flight away, the capital, Ambon (on Ambon island) has an almost equal population of Christian and Muslim inhabitants, and diverse cultural influences including Arab, Chinese and Dutch. Expect idyllic beaches, smouldering volcanoes and deliciously spicy seafood.

Ambon is accessible by sea, or air from Jakarta, Denpasar and Makassar.

CULTURAL TOURISM

Jogjakarta

One of Java's two royal cities (the other is Surakarta or Solo), Jogjakarta is also known as Yogyakarta but is usually shortened to Jogja. In many ways it represents

Indonesia (or at least Java) in a nutshell: temples, handicrafts, an active volcano, rugged beaches and many cultural activities. Must-see sights include the Borobudur (Buddhist) and Prambanan (Hindu) temples, the Kaliurang hill station on Mount **Merapi**, Parangtritis beach and the sultan's palace, the kraton. There are also numerous museums such as the Affandi art museum, batik and silver workshops, and the pottery village Kasongan. Jogja is an ideal city to explore by bicycle as it is flat and not too large. The main drag, Malioboro, houses not only a street market but also pop-up food vendors and eateries after dark, where you can enjoy specialties such as **gudeg** (cooked jackfruit). **Bakpia** cakes are another local treat.

Jogja is served by several flights a day from Jakarta. The train trip there from Jakarta, Bandung and Surabaya (all approximately 8 hours) is also pleasant.

FOOD

Medan
Indonesia's fifth-largest and often forgotten city, Medan boasts Malay, Arab, Chinese and Indian influences. This can be seen from the eclectic range of buildings in the old part of town—Chinese temples, the Little India food arcade, the fading glory of the Maimun palace, and old Dutch buildings along Kesawan. While the temperature is hot, Medan offers the visitor a bonus in terms of cu-

linary delights: flaky **roti jala**, noodles, **martabak** omelette, **lontong sayur** and **bika ambon** cakes. Medan is a good starting point for trips to the orangutans at Bukit Lawang, the hill town of Brastagi and Lake Toba.

There are flights to Medan from Singapore, Kuala Lumpur and Jakarta, as well as ferries from the Malaysian mainland.

PART FOUR

English–Indonesian Glossary

[A]

access	**aksés**
across, facing	**seberang**
active	**aktif**
after	**sesudah, habis**
again	**lagi**
agriculture	**pertanian**
air	**udara**
aircraft; machine	**pesawat**
airport	**bandara**
allergy	**alérgi**
alley, passage	**lorong, gang**
allowed (= may)	**boléh**
alone, by oneself, itself	**sendiri**
already, denotes past	**sudah**
already, denotes past (formal)	**telah**
animal	**binatang**
antibiotics	**antibiotik**
appropriate	**pantas, cocok**
approximately	**kira-kira**
April	**bulan April**
arm	**lengan, tangan**
around	**sekitar; kira-kira**
arrive, come	**datang, tiba**
arrival	**kedatangan**

ask, request, please	**minta**
at, on (of time)	**pada**
ATM	**ATM** [*ah te em*]
attire, clothing	**busana**
attractive	**menarik**
August	**bulan Agustus**
Australia	**Australia, Ustrali**
avocado	**alpukat**
[B]	
baby	**bayi**
back (= behind)	**belakang**
bag	**tas**
baggage, luggage	**bagasi**
ballpoint pen, biro	**bolpoin**
banana	**pisang**
base (= foundation)	**dasar**
basin, vat, trough	**bak**
bassinet, cradle	**basinét**
bathroom	**kamar mandi, kamar kecil**
battery	**baterai**
be able to	**bisa, dapat**
be able to speak a language	**berbahasa**
be careful	**hati-hati**
beef	**daging sapi**
before	**sebelum**
behind	**(di) belakang**
below	**(di) bawah**
belt	**ikat pinggang**
beside	**(di) samping**
between	**(di) antara**
bicycle, bike	**sepéda**

big, large	**besar**
birthday	**hari ulang tahun**
bite	**menggigit** (verb); **gigitan** (noun)
bitter	**pahit**
black	**hitam**
blister	**luka lécét**
blood	**darah**
blouse	**blus**
blue	**biru**
boarding house	**losmén**
book	**buku**
booking	**buking, pemesanan**
born	**lahir**
both	**sama-sama, semua, kedua-duanya**
boyfriend/girlfriend	**pacar**
bra, brassiere	**béha, kutang**
bread	**roti**
breakfast	**sarapan**
breastfeed, nurse	**menyusui**
bridge	**jembatan**
briefly (= for a while)	**sebentar**
bring	**bawa (membawa)**
broken	**rusak**
Buddhist/Hindu temple	**candi**
Buginese (people of South Sulawési)	**(orang) Bugis**
build	**bangun**
building	**gedung**
bus	**bis**
bus station	**términal**

business	**bisnis, usaha**
but	**tapi, tetapi**
button	**kancing**
buy	**beli (membeli)**

[C]

cable	**kabel**
can (= be able to)	**bisa, dapat**
capital (city)	**ibukota**
car	**mobil**
card	**kartu**
carousel	**korsél**
carrot	**wortel**
carry	**bawa (membawa)**
carving	**ukiran**
cave, tunnel	**gua**
cellphone	**ponsél**
cellphone (slang)	**hapé / HP** [*ha pe*]
cellphone credit	**pulsa**
center	**pusat**
cereal, muesli	**séréal**
charge (a device)	**ngecas**
cheap, inexpensive	**murah**
cheese	**kéju**
child, children	**anak, anak-anak**
China	**Tiongkok**
China (informal)	**Cina**
Chinese (person)	**(orang) Tionghoa, (orang) Cina**
Chinese New Year	**Imlék**
Chinese temple	**klénténg, kuil**
chip, cracker	**keripik**
chocolate; brown	**cokelat**

church	**géréja**
cigarette	**rokok**
city hall	**balaikota**
city, town	**kota**
clear (of weather)	**cerah**
climb up on, rise	**naik**
close, nearby	**dekat**
cloth, fabric	**kain**
clothes; shirt	**baju**
clothing	**pakaian**
cloudy, overcast	**mendung, berawan**
coconut	**kelapa**
code, password	**sandi**
coffee	**kopi**
cold, cool	**dingin**
cold, runny nose	**pilek**
coldsore, mouth ulcer	**sariawan**
collect (someone)	**jemput**
colonization	**penjajahan**
colonize	**menjajah**
color	**warna**
come, arrive	**datang, tiba**
come back	**kembali, balik**
come from	**berasal**
come in	**masuk**
comma	**koma**
company	**perusahaan**
computer	**komputer**
conditioner	**kondisioner, pelembab**
congratulations	**selamat**
constipated	**sembelit**
consult a doctor	**berobat**

contact lenses	**lénsa kontak**
continually	**terus-menerus**
cook (verb)	**memasak**
cool	**sejuk**
cost, fare	**ongkos**
cost, fee	**biaya**
cotton	**katun**
counter for baggage	**koli**
country	**negara**
cow, beef	**sapi**
crab	**kepiting**
cream	**krim**
crossing	**penyeberangan**
crossroads, intersection	**simpang, perempatan**
cucumber	**mentimun, timun**
cup noodles	**pop mie**
cuisine	**masakan**
[D]	
date	**tanggal**
day	**hari**
(the) day after tomorrow	**lusa**
(the) day before yesterday	**kemarin dulu**
(the) other day	**kemarin**
December	**bulan Désémber**
depart, leave	**berangkat**
department store	**tosérba**
departure	**keberangkatan**
destination	**tujuan**
diabetic, diabetes	**diabét**
diarrhea	**diaré, méncrét**
dictionary	**kamus**
die (of people)	**meninggal**

die, go out, turned off	**mati**
dipper, scoop (for washing)	**gayung**
directly	**langsung**
disappear	**hilang**
discard	**buang**
discount	**diskon**
divorced, divorce	**cerai**
docket	**struk, bon**
doctor	**dokter**
doll, soft toy	**bonéka**
dollar	**dolar**
don't	**jangan**
door, gate	**pintu**
dress; skirt	**rok**
drink (noun)	**minuman**
drink (verb)	**minum**
drizzle, light rain	**gerimis**
dry	**kering**
dry season	**kemarau**
Dutch; Holland, the Netherlands	**Belanda**

[E]

each	**masing-masing**
ear	**telinga**
earlier	**tadi**
early evening	**soré**
earring	**anting, giwang**
earthquake	**gempa (bumi)**
east	**timur**
eat	**makan**
effort; business	**usaha**
Eid ul Fitr, Islamic festival	**Lebaran, Idul Fitri**
eight	**delapan**

electronic	**éléktronik**
elementary school	**Sekolah Dasar (SD)**
eleven	**sebelas**
embroidery	**sulaman**
English, the UK, England	**Inggris**
enter, come in	**masuk**
envelope	**amplop**
era	**jaman**
evening, night	**malam**
exactly, just; fitting	**persis; pas**
exchange rate	**kurs**
exchange, trade, swap (verb)	**tukar**
excuse me	**permisi**
exit	**keluar**
expensive, dear	**mahal**
express	**éksprés**
expression, saying	**ungkapan**
eye drops	**tétés mata**
eye, eyes	**mata**
[F]	
Facebook	**fésbuk**
false, fake	**palsu**
fan (electric)	**kipas (angin)**
fare	**ongkos**
family	**keluarga, saudara**
farewell (verb)	**pamit**
farmer	**petani**
farming	**tani, pertanian**
father	**ayah**
father, older man	**bapak**
fax, facsimile	**faks, faksimili**
February	**bulan Fébruari**

fee	**biaya**
female, women	**wanita, perempuan**
fever	**demam**
finished, used up, sold out; after	**habis**
fire	**kebakaran**
first	**pertama**
first (among others)	**duluan**
first; before, in the past	**dulu**
fish	**ikan**
fitting	**pas**
five	**lima**
flight	**penerbangan**
floor, level, story	**lantai**
flower	**bunga**
flush, rinse	**siram**
fly (verb)	**terbang**
fog, mist	**kabut**
following, next	**berikut**
food	**makanan**
food, cooking, cuisine	**masakan**
foot, leg	**kaki**
for	**untuk, buat**
forbidden	**dilarang**
foundation	**dasar**
four	**empat**
free (of charge)	**gratis**
Friday	**hari Jumat**
fried	**goréng**
friend	**kawan, teman**
from	**dari**
front, before	**(di) depan**
fruit juice	**sari buah, jus**

fruit, fruits	**buah-buahan**
fruit; counter for objects	**buah**
fungus; mushroom	**jamur**

[G]

garage, workshop	**béngkél**
garden, park	**kebun, taman**
gate	**pintu**
general	**umum**
get	**dapat, terima**
glasses	**kacamata**
gloves, mittens	**kaus tangan, sarung tangan**
go	**pergi**
go by	**naik**
go crazy, run amok	**mengamuk**
go for a walk	**jalan-jalan**
go home, come home	**pulang**
go on, ride	**naik, menaiki**
go out (fire, power)	**mati**
gold, golden	**emas**
good (of objects)	**bagus**
Good Friday	**Jumat Agung**
good, well (of abstract things)	**baik**
government	**pemerintah**
grape; wine	**anggur**
green	**hijau**
guide	**panduan; pemandu**

[H]

half	**separuh, setengah**
handicraft	**kerajinan**
hat	**topi**
have	**ada, punya**

have to	**harus**
he, she, it	**dia**
head	**kepala**
hear	**dengar**
heirloom	**pusaka**
hello	**halo**
help; please (requesting assistance)	**tolong**
here	**di sini**
hero, heroine	**pahlawan**
Hindu temple	**pura**
hire, rent	**séwa**
historic, historical	**bersejarah**
honey	**madu**
hot	**panas; hangat**
hotel	**hotél**
hour	**jam**
house	**rumah**
how	**bagaimana**
how many, how much	**berapa**
hungry	**lapar**
husband	**suami**

[I]

I (familiar)	**aku**
I, me	**saya**
ice (cream)	**és krim**
if	**kalau**
import (verb)	**mendatangkan, mengimpor**
in, at	**di**
in, inside	**(di) dalam**
including	**termasuk**

Indonesia	**Indonésia**
injury	**luka**
instant	**instan**
interesting	**menarik**
international	**internasional**
international (phone call)	**SLI**
Internet	**internét**
Internet cafe	**warnét (warung internét)**
intersection	**simpang, perempatan**
iron (verb)	**menyetrika**
it	**dia**
Italy, Italian	**Itali, Italia**
[J]	
jacket	**jakét**
jail, prison	**penjara**
January	**bulan Januari**
Japan, Japanese	**Jepang**
Java, Javanese	**Jawa**
jelly	**agar-agar**
jellyfish	**ubur-ubur**
jewelry	**perhiasan**
juice	**jus, sari buah**
July	**bulan Juli**
June	**bulan Juni**
junior high school	**Sekolah Menengah Pertama (SMP)**
just	**saja, hanya, baru**
just now, earlier	**tadi**
[K]	
key, lock	**kunci**
keyring	**gantungan kunci**
kilogram, kilometer	**kilo**

king	**raja**
kingdom	**kerajaan**
know	**tahu; kenal** (a person)
know by heart	**hafal**
[L]	
lamp	**lampu**
language	**bahasa**
large	**besar**
late afternoon, early evening	**soré**
later	**nanti**
laundry (commercial)	**binatu, waserai**
lazy	**malas**
leg	**kaki**
less, not so	**kurang**
let's; please	**mari**
light, not heavy	**ringan**
light	**lampu**
lightning	**petir, halilintar**
likewise, same to you	**sama-sama**
listen	**dengar, dengarkan**
little	**kecil**
live, stay	**tinggal**
local	**lokal**
long (in length)	**panjang**
long (time), slow	**lama**
long-distance (phone call)	**interlokal, SLJJ**
look for, search for, seek	**cari, mencari**
lost, disappear	**hilang**
[M]	
made in, product of	**buatan**
magazine	**majalah**
make	**buat**

Malay	**Melayu**
male, men	**pria, laki-laki, lelaki**
mall, shopping center	**mal, pusat perbelanjaan**
many, lots	**banyak**
map	**peta**
March	**bulan Maret**
market	**pasar**
marry, (get) married	**nikah, kawin**
mask	**topéng, masker**
material; fabric	**bahan; kain**
May	**bulan Méi**
may	**boléh**
maybe	**mungkin**
meat, flesh	**daging**
medicine	**obat**
member	**anggota**
memorized, know by heart	**hafal**
menstruation	**méns, datang bulan**
message	**pesan**
middle	**tengah**
migraine	**(sakit kepala) migrén**
milk	**susu**
missed call	**miskol**
mittens	**kaus tangan, sarung tangan**
moisturiser	**pelembab**
(the) Moluccas	**Maluku**
moment	**saat**
Monday	**hari Senin**
money	**uang**
month; moon	**bulan**
more	**lebih**

mosque	**mesjid**
mosquito	**nyamuk**
mosquito coil	**koil**
most (superlative)	**paling**
mother	**ibu**
motorcycle taxi	**ojék**
mouth ulcer	**sariawan**
move (house)	**pindah**
museum	**musium**
must, have to	**harus**
[N]	
name	**nama**
nation, country	**negara, negeri**
nearby	**dekat**
necklace	**kalung**
need	**perlu**
new	**baru**
news	**berita, kabar**
newspaper	**koran, surat kabar**
next	**berikut**
next to, beside	**(di) sebelah, (di) samping**
night	**malam**
nine	**sembilan**
no	**tidak**
no need, not necessary	**tidak usah**
no, not (of objects)	**bukan**
noble	**mulia**
noodles	**mie**
north	**utara**
nose	**hidung**
not	**tidak**
not necessary	**tidak usah**

not yet	**belum**
novel	**roman**
November	**bulan Novémber**
now	**sekarang**
number	**nomor; angka; jumlah**
nuts	**kacang, kacang-kacangan**

[O]

occupation, colonization	**penjajahan**
October	**bulan Oktober**
office	**kantor**
old; dark (of colors)	**tua**
older brother or sister	**kakak**
on (top)	**atas**
once, one time; very	**sekali**
one	**satu, se-**
one half	**sebelah, separuh, setengah**
only	**hanya, saja**
open; take off	**buka**
or	**atau**
orange, mandarin	**jeruk**
other	**lain**
out, exit	**keluar**
outside	**(di) luar**
over there	**di sana**
overcast	**mendung**

[P]

package (of food)	**bungkus**
packet, package	**pakét**
painful	**sakit**
painting	**lukisan**
pair	**pasang**
palace	**istana, puri**

pants, trousers	**celana**
paracetamol (painkiller)	**parasétamol**
park	**taman**
password	**sandi, kata kunci**
past	**léwat, lalu**
pay	**bayar (membayar)**
pedicab	**bécak**
pen, ballpoint, biro	**péna**
per	**per**
period, era, time	**jaman**
period, menstruation	**méns, datang bulan**
person	**orang**
pharmacy	**apoték, apotik**
phrase	**frasa**
pick up, collect (someone)	**jemput**
pickpocket	**copét**
pig	**babi**
place	**tempat**
play	**main, bermain**
please (inviting someone)	**silahkan**
please (offering to someone)	**coba**
please (requesting assistance)	**tolong**
pollution	**polusi**
pond, pool	**kolam**
pork	**daging babi**
porter	**kuli**
Portugal, Portuguese	**Portugal, Portugis**
possible, maybe	**mungkin**
post	**pos**
pot (ceramic ~)	**tembikar**
pound sterling (£)	**pon stérling**
prefix making the verb passive	**di-**

pregnant	**hamil**
prescription; recipe	**resép**
price	**harga**
prince	**pangeran**
princess	**permaisuri, putri**
print (out)	**cétak, mencétak, ngeprint**
prison	**penjara**
public, general	**umum**
[Q]	
quarter	**perempat, seperempat**
queen	**ratu**
[R]	
rain	**hujan**
rash	**ruam, gatal-gatal**
receive, get	**dapat, terima**
reception	**résépsi**
recipe	**resep**
registered	**tercatat**
relation, sibling	**saudara**
repeat	**ulang**
reservation	**résérvasi**
rest	**istirahat**
restaurant	**rumah makan, réstoran**
restroom, bathroom	**toilét, WC, kamar kechil**
return, come back	**kembali**
rice (cooked)	**nasi**
ride, go by, climb up on, rise	**naik**
ring	**cincin**
rise	**naik**
road, street	**jalan**
roadside stall	**warung**
roll	**gulung**

room	**kamar**
roughly, approximately	**kira-kira**

[S]

safe, secure	**aman, selamat**
salty, savory	**asin**
same	**sama**
same to you	**sama-sama**
sandals	**sepatu sendal**
sanitary napkin/pad	**pembalut**
sarong	**sarung**
sash, shawl	**seléndang**
satellite dish	**parabola**
sausage	**sosis**
savory	**asin**
saying	**ungkapan, peribahasa**
school	**sekolah**
sea	**laut**
season	**musim**
secure	**aman**
security	**keamanan**
seed; counter for small objects	**biji**
self-service grocery, supermarket	**swalayan**
sell	**jual, menjual**
send	**kirim**
senior high school	**Sekolah Menengah Atas (SMA)**
separate, part	**pisah**
September	**bulan Séptémber**
service	**pelayanan, jasa**
service, repairs	**sérvis**
seven	**tujuh**
shadow puppet	**wayang**

shampoo	**sampo**
she	**dia**
shell, mollusc	**kerang**
shirt	**baju**
shirt (with collar)	**keméja**
shirt, T-shirt	**kaus**
shoe, shoes	**sepatu**
shop	**toko**
shophouse	**ruko (rumah toko)**
shopping	**belanja**
shopping center	**mal, pusat perbelanjaan**
shops	**pertokoan**
shorts, short pants	**celana péndék**
sibling	**saudara, kakak/adik**
sick, ill, unwell, painful	**sakit**
signal	**sinyal**
silk	**sutera**
silver	**pérak**
Singapore	**Singapura**
sit	**duduk**
six	**enam**
skin, leather	**kulit**
skirt	**rok**
sleep	**tidur**
slow	**lambat**
slowly	**pelan-pelan, perlahan-lahan**
small, little	**kecil**
smoke	**asap**
smoke (verb)	**merokok**
snow	**salju**

soap, detergent	**sabun**
social	**sosial**
social media	**sosméd, médsos**
socks	**kaus kaki**
sold out	**habis**
something	**sesuatu**
soon	**segera, sebentar lagi**
sorry	**maaf**
sour	**asam**
souvenir	**oléh-oléh**
speak, talk	**bicara**
speed, race	**ngebut**
stair, ladder	**tangga**
stall, outlet	**kedai**
star	**bintang**
station (railway)	**setasiun**
stay	**tinggal**
stick; counter for cigarettes	**batang**
sticking plaster	**pléster, hansaplast**
still	**masih**
sting	**gigitan, sengatan**
stone, rock	**batu**
stop	**berhenti, setop**
storm	**badai**
straight	**terus**
strawberry	**strobéri**
street, road	**jalan**
strong	**kuat**
study, learn	**belajar**
suck	**isap**
sugar	**gula**
suitable, appropriate	**cocok, pantas**

suitcase	**koper**
Sumatra	**Sumatera**
sunblock, sunscreen	**tabir surya**
Sunday	**hari Minggu**
supermarket	**swalayan, supermarkét**
swap	**tukar**
sweet	**manis**
sweet, candy	**permén**
swimming	**renang**
synthetic, nylon	**sintétis**

[T]

table	**méja**
tail	**ékor**
take	**ambil (mengambil);** **antar, antarkan**
take leave, farewell	**pamit**
take off	**buka**
take time	**makan waktu**
tap, faucet	**keran**
tariff, rate, charge	**tarif**
taximeter	**argo**
tea	**téh**
telecommunications	**télékomunikasi**
telephone	**télépon**
telephone office	**wartél**
television	**télévisi**
tempeh	**tempé**
ten	**sepuluh**
terminal, terminus, bus station	**términal**
test, quiz	**tés**
text message	**SMS**
thank you	**terima kasih**

that	**itu; bahwa**
the ..., (denotes possessive)	**-nya**
there is/are; have	**ada**
thermos	**térmos**
they, them	**meréka**
this	**ini**
thousand	**ribu**
thread	**benang**
three	**tiga**
throat	**tenggorokan**
trousers	**celana**
throw away, discard	**buang**
thunder	**geludug, guntur**
ticket	**karcis, tiket**
tie	**dasi**
tile (ceramic)	**ubin, keramik**
time; when	**waktu**
tissue, toilet paper	**tisu**
to	**ke, kepada** (someone)
today	**hari ini**
tofu	**tahu**
together	**bersama**
toilet, restroom, bathroom	**toilét, WC, kamar kecil**
toll (road)	**(jalan) tol**
tomorrow; in the future	**bésok**
tool, instrument	**alat**
tooth, teeth	**gigi**
tourism	**pariwisata, wisata**
town square (in Java)	**alun-alun**
toy	**mainan**
train	**keréta, keréta api**
trolley	**troli**

try; please (offering to someone)	**coba**
tunnel	**terowongan; gua**
turn (direction)	**bélok**
turn, rotate, spin	**putar**
turned off	**mati**
tweet (on Twitter)	**ngetwit**
two	**dua**
typhoid fever	**tifus, tipus**

[U]

umbrella, parasol	**payung**
under	**(di) bawah**
understand	**mengerti**
university student	**mahasiswa**
until	**sampai**
unwell	**sakit**
urinate, defecate	**buang air**
USA	**Amérika (Serikat, AS)**
use, wear; with	**pakai**
used up	**habis**

[V]

vegetables	**sayur, sayur-sayuran**
vegetarian	**végétarian**
very	**sangat, sekali**
via, through; past	**léwat**
view	**pemandangan**

[W]

waist, middle	**pinggang**
wait	**tunggu**
wake or get up	**bangun**
walk, go	**jalan**
wallet, purse	**dompét**
want, will	**mau**

war	**perang**
warm	**hangat**
wash (clothes, dishes)	**cuci**
wash (your body), bathe	**mandi**
water; juice	**air**
watermelon	**semangka**
way, direction	**arah**
we, us (excluding person addressed)	**kami**
we, us (including person addressed)	**kita**
weather	**cuaca**
weaving, woven cloth	**tenunan, ikat**
week	**minggu**
west	**barat**
what	**apa, kenapa** (informal)
when	**kapan** (question); **ketika**
where; which	**mana**
whether	**apakah**
which, that	**yang**
why?	**mengapa, kenapa**
white	**putih**
who	**siapa**
wife	**isteri**
wind	**angin**
window	**jendéla**
wish, want, would like	**ingin**
with	**dengan, pakai**
without	**tanpa**
women	**wanita, perempuan**
word	**kata**
work	**kerja, perkerjaan**

work (verb)	**bekerja**
work, creation	**karya**
workshop	**béngkél**
write	**tulis**

[Y]

year	**tahun**
yes	**ya**
yesterday, the other day	**kemarin**
you (familiar)	**kamu, engkau, kau**
you (neutral)	**anda**
you (plural)	**kalian**
you (to an older woman)	**Ibu**
you (to older man)	**Bapak**
young; light (of colors)	**muda**
younger brother or sister	**adik**

[Z]

zone, area	**kawasan**

Published by Tuttle Publishing, an imprint of
Periplus Editions (HK) Ltd.

www.tuttlepublishing.com

Copyright © 2016 Periplus Editions (HK) Ltd.

Library of Congress Control Number:
2015953682

ISBN 978-0-8048-4523-6

20 19 18 17 16   5 4 3 2 1   1512CP
Printed in Singapore

Distributed by:
North America, Latin America & Europe
Tuttle Publishing
364 Innovation Drive
North Clarendon, VT 05759-9436 U.S.A.
Tel: 1 (802) 773-8930; Fax: 1 (802) 773-6993
info@tuttlepublishing.com
www.tuttlepublishing.com

Japan
Tuttle Publishing
Yaekari Building, 3rd Floor, 5-4-12 Osaki,
Shinagawa-ku, Tokyo 141 0032
Tel: (81) 3 5437-0171; Fax: (81) 3 5437-0755
sales@tuttle.co.jp
www.tuttle.co.jp

Asia Pacific
Berkeley Books Pte. Ltd.
61 Tai Seng Avenue #02-12
Singapore 534167
Tel: (65) 6280-1330; Fax: (65) 6280-6290
inquiries@periplus.com.sg
www.periplus.com

ABOUT TUTTLE
"Books to Span the East and West"

Our core mission at Tuttle Publishing
is to create books which bring
people together one page at a
time. Tuttle was founded in 1832
in the small New England town of
Rutland, Vermont (USA). Our fun-
damental values remain as strong
today as they were then—to pub-
lish best-in-class books informing
the English-speaking world about
the countries and peoples of Asia.
The world has become a smaller
place today and Asia's economic,
cultural and political influence has
expanded, yet the need for mean-
ingful dialogue and information
about this diverse region has never
been greater. Since 1948, Tuttle
has been a leader in publishing
books on the cultures, arts, cuisines,
languages and literatures of Asia.
Our authors and photographers
have won numerous awards and
Tuttle has published thousands of
books on subjects ranging from
martial arts to paper crafts. We
welcome you to explore the wealth
of information available on Asia at
www.tuttlepublishing.com.